NATURAL DISASTER RESEARCH, PREDICTION AND MITIGATION

FLOOD AND HOMEOWNERS INSURANCE

CONSIDERATIONS FOR EXPANDING THE ROLE OF PRIVATE INSURERS

NATURAL DISASTER RESEARCH, PREDICTION AND MITIGATION

Additional books in this series can be found on Nova's website under the Series tab.

Additional e-books in this series can be found on Nova's website under the e-book tab.

NATURAL DISASTER RESEARCH, PREDICTION AND MITIGATION

FLOOD AND HOMEOWNERS INSURANCE

CONSIDERATIONS FOR EXPANDING THE ROLE OF PRIVATE INSURERS

ELLA GRACE IRWIN
EDITOR

NOVINKA

New York

For permission to use material from this book please contact us:
Telephone 631-231-7269; Fax 631-231-8175
Web Site: http://www.novapublishers.com

Library of Congress Cataloging-in-Publication Data

ISBN: 978-1-63117-888-7

Published by Nova Science Publishers, Inc. † New York

CONTENTS

PREFACE

According to stakeholders with whom the United States Government Accountability office spoke, several conditions must be present to increase private sector involvement in the sale of flood insurance. First, insurers need to be able to accurately assess risk to determine premium rates. Second, insurers need to be able to charge premium rates that reflect the full estimated risk of potential flood losses while still allowing the companies to make a profit, as well as be able to decide which applicants they will insure. However, stakeholders said that such rates might seem unaffordable to many homeowners. Third, insurers need sufficient consumer participation to properly manage and diversify their risk, but stakeholders said that many property owners do not buy flood insurance because they may have an inaccurate perception of their risk of flooding. This book addresses the conditions needed for private sector involvement in flood insurance and strategies for increasing private sector involvement.

Chapter 1 – NFIP has accrued $24 billion in debt, highlighting structural weaknesses in the program and increasing concerns about its burden on taxpayers. As a result, some have suggested shifting exposure to the private sector and eliminating subsidized premium rates, so individual property owners—not taxpayers—would pay for their risk of flood loss. NFIP was created, in part, because private insurers were unwilling to insure against flood damage, but new technologies and a better understanding of flood risks may have increased their willingness to offer flood coverage.

The Biggert-Waters Flood Insurance Reform Act of 2012 moves NFIP toward charging more full-risk rates. It also mandates that GAO conduct a study on increasing private sector involvement in flood insurance. This report addresses (1) the conditions needed for private sector involvement in flood insurance and (2) strategies for increasing private sector involvement. To do this work, GAO reviewed available documentation and hosted a roundtable in August 2013 that included stakeholders from FEMA, the insurance and reinsurance industries, and state insurance regulators, among others. GAO also interviewed other similar stakeholders.

Chapter 2 – Homeowners insurance protects against a range of perils, but policies do not insure against all risks. Owners whose homes are damaged by natural and other disasters not covered by their insurance can be exposed to serious financial losses. Federal and state initiatives provide some assistance for catastrophes, which can involve significant taxpayer expense. With coastal populations growing and the possibility of more frequent and severe weather, more homeowners could experience heavy losses not covered by homeowners insurance, putting increasing financial pressure on government programs and thus on taxpayers.

GAO was asked to study the possibility of private insurers providing more comprehensive insurance. This report addresses (1) what perils homeowners policies typically cover and exclude, (2) how exclusions impact homeowners and taxpayers and the potential benefits of more comprehensive coverage, and (3) what additional perils insurers might be willing to cover and what challenges are associated with expanding policies. GAO reviewed homeowners insurance policies and conducted interviews with the National Association of Insurance Commissioners, other industry organizations, consumer advocates, and risk experts, among others.

In: Flood and Homeowners Insurance
Editor: Ella Grace Irwin

ISBN: 978-1-63117-888-7

Chapter 1

FLOOD INSURANCE: STRATEGIES FOR INCREASING PRIVATE SECTOR INVOLVEMENT*

United States Government Accountability Office

WHY GAO DID THIS STUDY

NFIP has accrued $24 billion in debt, highlighting structural weaknesses in the program and increasing concerns about its burden on taxpayers. As a result, some have suggested shifting exposure to the private sector and eliminating subsidized premium rates, so individual property owners—not taxpayers—would pay for their risk of flood loss. NFIP was created, in part, because private insurers were unwilling to insure against flood damage, but new technologies and a better understanding of flood risks may have increased their willingness to offer flood coverage.

The Biggert-Waters Flood Insurance Reform Act of 2012 moves NFIP toward charging more full-risk rates. It also mandates that GAO conduct a study on increasing private sector involvement in flood insurance. This report addresses (1) the conditions needed for private sector involvement in flood insurance and (2) strategies for increasing private sector involvement. To do this work, GAO reviewed available documentation and hosted a roundtable in

* This is an edited, reformatted and augmented version of the United States Government Accountability Office publication, GAO-14-127, dated January 2014.

August 2013 that included stakeholders from FEMA, the insurance and reinsurance industries, and state insurance regulators, among others. GAO also interviewed other similar stakeholders.

What GAO Recommends

While GAO makes no new recommendations in this report, GAO reiterates its previous suggestion from a June 2011 report (GAO-11-297) that Congress consider eliminating subsidized rates, charge full-risk rates to all policyholders, and appropriate funds for premium assistance to eligible policyholders to address affordability issues.

What GAO Found

According to stakeholders with whom GAO spoke, several conditions must be present to increase private sector involvement in the sale of flood insurance. First, insurers need to be able to accurately assess risk to determine premium rates. For example, stakeholders told GAO that access to National Flood Insurance Program (NFIP) policy and claims data and upcoming improvements in private sector computer modeling could enable them to better assess risk. Second, insurers need to be able to charge premium rates that reflect the full estimated risk of potential flood losses while still allowing the companies to make a profit, as well as be able to decide which applicants they will insure. However, stakeholders said that such rates might seem unaffordable to many homeowners. Third, insurers need sufficient consumer participation to properly manage and diversify their risk, but stakeholders said that many property owners do not buy flood insurance because they may have an inaccurate perception of their risk of flooding.

Stakeholders identified several strategies that could help create conditions that would promote the sale of flood insurance by the private sector. For example,

- *NFIP charging full-risk rates.* Congress could eliminate subsidized rates, charge all policyholders full-risk rates, and appropriate funding for a direct means-based subsidy to some policyholders. Stakeholders said full-risk NFIP rates would encourage private sector participation because they would be much closer to the rates private insurers would need to charge. The explicit subsidy would address affordability concerns, increase transparency, and reduce taxpayer costs depending on the extent and amount of the subsidy. The Biggert-Waters Act eliminates some subsidized rates, but some have proposed delaying these rate increases. Doing so could address affordability concerns, but would also delay addressing NFIP's burden on taxpayers.

- *NFIP providing residual insurance.* The federal government could also encourage private sector involvement by providing coverage for the highest- risk properties that the private sector is unwilling to insure. Providing residual coverage could increase the program's exposure relative to the number of properties it insured, but NFIP would be insuring fewer properties, and charging adequate rates could reduce taxpayer costs.
- *NFIP as reinsurer.* Alternatively, the federal government could serve as a reinsurer, charging a premium for assuming the risk of catastrophic losses. However, the cost of reinsurance premiums would likely be passed on to consumers, with higher rates potentially decreasing consumer participation.

Stakeholders identified other strategies including mandatory coverage requirements to ensure broad participation, NFIP purchasing reinsurance from the private sector rather than borrowing from the U.S. Treasury, and NFIP issuing catastrophe bonds to transfer risk to private investors. As the private sector increases its role in providing flood coverage, the federal government could collaborate with state and local governments to focus on other important roles, including promoting risk awareness among consumers, encouraging mitigation, enforcing building codes, overseeing land use agreements, and streamlining insurance regulations.

ABBREVIATIONS

Biggert-Waters Act	Biggert-Waters Flood Insurance Reform Act of 2012
FEMA	Federal Emergency Management Agency
FIRM	Flood Insurance Rate Map
HUD	U.S. Department of Housing and Urban Development

NFIP	National Flood Insurance Program
SFHA	Special Flood Hazard Area
Treasury	U.S. Department of the Treasury

January 22, 2014

The Honorable Tim Johnson
Chairman
The Honorable Mike Crapo
Ranking Member
Committee on Banking, Housing and Urban Affairs
United States Senate

The Honorable Jeb Hensarling
Chairman
The Honorable Maxine Waters
Ranking Member
Committee on Financial Services
House of Representatives

The National Flood Insurance Program (NFIP) is the key component of the federal government's efforts to minimize the damage floods cause and the resulting financial impact and is the only source of insurance against flood damage for most residents of flood-prone areas. Since 2000, NFIP has experienced several years with catastrophic losses, primarily from Hurricane Katrina and the other 2005 storms and Superstorm Sandy in 2012. Since then, the Federal Emergency Management Agency (FEMA), which administers NFIP, has needed to borrow money from the U.S. Department of the Treasury (Treasury) to cover claims in some years. As of September 2013, FEMA owed Treasury $24 billion—up from $17.8 billion prior to Superstorm Sandy—and had not repaid any principal on its loans since 2010.[1] NFIP is unlikely to be able to repay this debt in the near future, if ever.[2] Because of its recurring financial and management challenges, NFIP has been on our high-risk list since March 2006.[3]

NFIP's growing debt has highlighted structural weaknesses in the program and increased concerns about its burden on taxpayers. As a result, Congress has shown increased interest in reducing the federal government's role in flood insurance by transferring its exposure to the private sector. Flood insurance reform involves the question of who should be responsible for paying to insure against the flood risk that arises from living in a particular location—the individual property owners themselves, taxpayers, or some combination of the two. Unlike private insurance, which makes individuals responsible for their own risk through premiums that reflect that risk, NFIP relies in part on taxpayer money. Historically, NFIP was not designed to be actuarially sound, so premiums do not cover the program's costs. The National Flood Insurance Act of 1968 authorized subsidized rates to encourage participation in NFIP, especially for properties in high-risk locations that were built before Flood Insurance Rate Maps (FIRM) became available and the level of risk was clearly understood.[4] Without the subsidies, these properties would have been charged significantly higher premiums. FEMA estimates that about 1.1 million of 5.5 million NFIP policies—about 20 percent—have subsidized rates. The discounted premiums encourage property owners to join the program but do not provide enough revenue to cover potential losses, and many subsidized policies have had high losses.[5]

The Biggert-Waters Flood Insurance Reform Act of 2012 (Biggert-Waters Act) reauthorized NFIP through 2017 and made some significant changes, such as eliminating the subsidies for certain properties, creating a reserve fund, and eliminating the grandfathering of properties at old rates after remapping.[6] These changes are important steps in putting NFIP on the path toward financial solvency, but a number of policies will continue to receive subsidized rates. This report addresses one of several GAO mandates in the Biggert-Waters Act: to assess a broad range of options, methods, and strategies for privatizing NFIP.[7] The report discusses (1) conditions needed for private sector involvement in flood insurance and (2) strategies for increasing such involvement.

To address these objectives, we reviewed NFIP laws, regulations, and history, FEMA reports, academic studies, our prior work on NFIP, and other documentation and reports. We also interviewed a variety of stakeholders and held a roundtable in August 2013 to obtain views on increasing private sector involvement in flood insurance. Stakeholders participating in interviews and the roundtable included representatives from FEMA, the Federal Insurance Office, private insurers, reinsurers, state residual insurance programs, state insurance regulators, actuaries, insurance adjusters, insurance agents, a catastrophe modeling firm, consumer advocates, floodplain managers, mortgage bankers, realtors, an academic, and other experts.

We conducted this performance audit from March 2013 to January 2014 in accordance with generally accepted government auditing standards. Those standards require that we plan and perform the audit to obtain sufficient, appropriate evidence to provide a reasonable basis for our findings and conclusions based on our audit objectives. We believe that the evidence obtained provides a reasonable basis for our findings and conclusions based on our audit objectives.

BACKGROUND

Floods are the most common and destructive natural disaster in the United States. However, flooding is generally excluded from homeowners insurance policies, which typically cover damages from other losses, such as wind, fire, and theft. Because of the catastrophic nature of flooding, the difficulty of adequately predicting flood risks, and uncertainty surrounding the possibility of charging actuarially sound premium rates, private insurance companies have historically been largely unwilling to underwrite flood insurance. NFIP, which makes federally backed flood insurance available to residential property owners and businesses, was intended to reduce the federal government's escalating costs for repairing flood damage after disasters. Under NFIP, the federal government currently assumes the liability for the insurance coverage and sets rates and coverage limitations, among other responsibilities, while private insurers sell the policies and administer the claims for a fee determined by FEMA. NFIP is managed by FEMA's Federal Insurance and Mitigation Administration, which is responsible for administering programs that provide assistance for mitigating future damages from natural hazards. Some private insurers provide coverage for flood insurance above the limit of NFIP coverage, generally referred to as excess flood insurance.[8] Further, NFIP policies do not provide coverage for business interruption or additional living expenses, which currently are available through some private insurers.

Community participation in NFIP is voluntary, but communities must join NFIP and adopt and enforce FEMA-approved building standards and floodplain management strategies in order for their residents to purchase flood insurance through the program. Additionally, communities in Special Flood Hazard Areas (SFHA)—areas subject to a 1 percent or greater chance of flooding in any given year—must participate in NFIP for property owners to be eligible for any aid in connection with a flood, including disaster assistance loans and grants for acquisition or construction purposes. Participating communities agree to enforce regulations for land use and new construction in high-risk flood zones and to adopt and enforce state and community floodplain management regulations to reduce future flood damage. Participating communities can receive discounts on flood insurance if they establish floodplain management programs that go beyond NFIP's minimum requirements.[9]

FEMA can suspend communities that do not comply with the program, and communities can withdraw from it by submitting a copy of a legislative action stating its desire to withdraw from NFIP. As of May 2013, about 22,000 communities voluntarily participated in NFIP.[10]

NFIP has mapped flood risks across the country, assigning flood zone designations based on risk levels, and these designations are a factor in determining premium rates. To help reduce or eliminate the long-term risk of flood damage to buildings and other structures insured by NFIP, FEMA has used a variety of mitigation efforts, such as elevation, relocation, and demolition. Despite these efforts, the number of repetitive loss properties—generally, those that have had two or more flood insurance claims payments of $1,000 or more over 10 years—has continued to grow.[11]

Subsidized Premium Rates

NFIP policies have what FEMA describes as either subsidized or full-risk premiums. The type of policy and the subsequent rate a policyholder pays depend on several property characteristics—for example, whether the structure was built before or after a community's FIRM was issued and the location of the structure in the floodplain. Structures built after a community's FIRM was published must meet FEMA building standards, and the property owner must pay full-risk rates, which reflect FEMA's estimates of the actual risk of flooding. Post-FIRM structures are generally less flood prone than pre-FIRM properties because they have been built to flood-resistant building codes or mitigation steps have been taken to reduce flood risks.

Subsidized rates do not reflect the estimated total flood risk and instead are highly discounted. Even with highly discounted rates, subsidized premiums are, on average, higher than full-risk premiums because subsidized pre-FIRM structures generally are more prone to flooding (that is, riskier) than other structures. In general, pre-FIRM properties were not constructed according to the program's building standards or were built without regard to base flood elevation—the level relative to mean sea level at which there is an estimated 1 percent or greater chance of flooding in a given year. For example, the average annual subsidized premium with October 2011 rates for pre-FIRM subsidized properties was about $1,224, while the average annual premium for post-FIRM properties paying full-risk rates was about $492.

Program History

Flooding disasters of the 1920s and 1930s led to federal involvement in protecting life and property from flooding, with the passage of the Flood Control Act of 1936.[12] Generally, the only available financial recourse to assist flood victims was postdisaster assistance. When flood insurance was first proposed in the 1950s, it became clear that private insurance companies could not profitably provide flood coverage at a price that consumers could afford, primarily because of the catastrophic nature of flooding and the difficulty of determining accurate rates.[13]

In 1965 Congress passed the Southeast Hurricane Disaster Relief Act that provided financial relief for victims of flooding.[14] In addition, the act mandated a feasibility study of a national flood insurance program, which helped provide the basis for the National Flood Insurance Act of 1968 that created NFIP.[15] From 1969 through 1977, the Department of Housing and Urban Development (HUD), which administered NFIP at the time, had an agreement with a consortium of private insurers known as the National Flood Insurers Association. Under this agreement, HUD reimbursed the association of insurers for operating costs and provided an annual operating allowance equal to 5 percent of policyholders' premiums. HUD ended the partnership in 1978 and converted NFIP to a government- operated program because it could not come to an agreement with the private insurers on issues such as HUD's right to approve their operating budgets and its authority over policy decisions and regulations. HUD also estimated $15 million in cost savings by ending the partnership. The insurers wanted to continue the partnership, but the HUD Secretary decided to use her statutory authority to convert NFIP to a government program. In 1978, we determined that the partnership had not reached a last resort status and that the potential for a new agreement existed.[16]

The Flood Disaster Protection Act of 1973 made the purchase of flood insurance mandatory for owners of properties in special flood hazard areas that are secured by mortgages from federally regulated lenders and provided additional incentives for communities to join the program.[17] The National Flood Insurance Reform Act of 1994—which amended the 1968 act and the 1973 act—strengthened the mandatory purchase requirements for owners of properties located in SFHAs with mortgages from federally regulated lenders.[18] The Bunning-Bereuter-Blumenauer Flood Insurance Reform Act of 2004 authorized a pilot program to encourage owners of properties that suffer from repeated flood losses to take steps to reduce the risk of damage, known as mitigation.[19] Owners of these "severe repetitive loss" properties who refuse an offer to mitigate the risks face higher premiums.

Finally, in 2012 the Biggert-Waters Act reauthorized the program through 2017 and removed subsidized rates for a number of insured properties, such as residential properties that are not an individual's primary residence, severe repetitive loss properties, business properties, and properties that had received payments for flood-related damage that cumulatively equaled or exceeded the property's fair market value.[20] The Biggert-Waters Act also included several other provisions, such as the following

- Rates that fully reflect flood risk for specified properties are to be phased in over several years—with increases of 25 percent each year—until the average risk premium rate for these properties equals the average of the full-risk premium rates for all properties in that risk classification.[21]
- Properties will no longer qualify for subsidies if the policyholder has deliberately chosen to let the policy lapse and if a prospective insured refuses to accept any offer of mitigation assistance (including relocation) following a major disaster.[22]
- Properties that did not have NFIP insurance when the act was enacted and properties purchased after that date will not receive subsidies. Subsidized properties that are sold will lose their subsidies.[23]
- FEMA must adjust rates to accurately reflect the current risk of flooding to properties when an area's flood map is changed.[24] FEMA is determining how this provision will affect properties that were grandfathered into lower rates.

In addition, the act allows average premium increases of 20 percent annually by risk class (the previous cap was 10 percent), establishes minimum deductibles, requires FEMA to establish a reserve fund, and requires FEMA to include losses from catastrophic years in determining premiums that are based on the "average historical loss year," among other things. The potential adverse effects on certain property owners of the premium rate increases arising out of the Biggert-Waters Act and the possibility of delaying some rate increases have been the subject of congressional hearings and recent legislative proposals.[25]

Policy Goals Framework

We previously identified goals for federal involvement in natural catastrophe insurance programs.[26] These goals can be adapted to help evaluate strategies for increasing private sector involvement in flood insurance. The goals include:

- charging premium rates that fully reflect estimated risks,
- encouraging private markets to provide flood insurance,
- encouraging property owners to buy flood insurance, and
- limiting costs to taxpayers before and after a flood.

The four-goal framework captures the public policy goals for providing insurance against natural catastrophes such as flooding. Stakeholders with whom we spoke generally agreed that these goals were appropriate.[27]

Stakeholders Identified Several Conditions That Must Exist to Encourage Private Sector Involvement in Flood Insurance

Stakeholders with whom we spoke or who participated in our roundtable discussion identified several conditions that would be needed to increase private sector involvement in flood insurance. First, private insurers would have to perceive floods as an insurable risk that they could profitably cover—that is, they would need to be able to estimate both the frequency and severity of future losses with some accuracy. Second, they would need the freedom to charge adequate rates and decide which applicants they would insure. Third, private insurers would need adequate consumer participation in order to manage and diversify their risk.

Private Insurers Must Be Able to Accurately Assess Flood Risk

Private insurers generally cover only what they see as insurable risks whose frequency and severity they can estimate with some accuracy. Being able to calculate the average frequency and severity of future losses enables insurers to set premium rates that are likely to be sufficient to pay all claims and expenses and yield a profit. For this reason, homeowners policies do not cover a variety of risks, such as flooding, which tend to occur unexpectedly and can cause a devastating amount of damage.[28] NFIP was created in part because the catastrophic nature of flooding made it difficult for private insurance companies to develop an actuarial rate structure that could adequately reflect the risks to flood-prone properties.[29] The program is the only provider of affordable flood insurance for most U.S. homeowners.

Stakeholders indicated that private insurers would need more information and more sophisticated modeling to assess flood risk before they could begin providing flood insurance.[30] Risk modelers with whom we spoke questioned the reliability of FEMA's flood risk zones, which in many areas, such as along coastlines, were determined using a less sophisticated methodology than what is available today. For example, one risk modeler said that FEMA's base flood elevations were likely too low in many places and that many structures across the country were at higher flood risk than the flood maps indicated. According to one insurer, determining flood risk for commercial policyholders involves reviewing specific information, including FEMA flood maps and satellite imagery, to determine a structure's flood zone, proximity to other flood zones, and elevation. This insurer uses geographical address information to determine flood risk on a building-by-building basis based on a range of factors that include the structural elements of a building and its contents. One risk modeler suggested that FEMA should design flood risk maps for future building stock and should model both current and future flood levels; however, the risk modeler said that determining future flood risks was a challenge and that the industry lacked consensus on the methodology that should be used.[31]

Stakeholders anticipated that risk modeling firms would be releasing new flood models in the next several years, providing the tools that private insurers would need to evaluate flood risk. Stakeholders also noted that a private market for flood insurance would likely create a market for modeling flood risk, attracting many companies to fill that need. Stakeholders said that if other conditions for private sector involvement in flood insurance were met, more risk-modeling companies or private insurers would begin developing models that private insurers could use to determine risks more accurately. For example, one risk modeler said risk modelers could determine how different bodies of water, such as two rivers, would interact and contribute to flood events—information that FEMA's flood maps do not include.

Stakeholders said that in addition to advanced computer modeling, access to NFIP policy and claims data would help private insurers assess flood risks and determine which properties they might be willing to insure. However,

FEMA officials said the agency would need to address privacy concerns to provide property-level information to insurers, because the Privacy Act prohibits the agency from releasing detailed NFIP policy and claims data. The Privacy Act governs how federal agencies may use the personal information that individuals supply when obtaining government services or fulfilling obligations.[32] FEMA officials said that while the agency could release data in the aggregate, some information could not be provided in detail. For example, FEMA could provide zip-code level information to communities but would need to determine how to release property-level information while protecting the privacy of individuals.

Private Insurers Would Need Freedom to Charge Adequate Rates and Manage Risk

Stakeholders said that private insurers would also need to be able to charge adequate rates that would reflect the full estimated risk of flood loss and allow for profit. In our prior work, one of the public policy goals we adapted for evaluating options for increasing private sector involvement in flood insurance was charging premium rates that fully reflected estimated risks.[33] Actuarially sound rates determined by private insurers would differ from NFIP rates in that they would be calculated to account for potential losses, reflect the cost of capital to cover potential catastrophic losses, and provide a reasonable return for investors. As a result, these rates would be higher than present NFIP rates for many properties and could present affordability challenges for consumers. One stakeholder said higher prices could lead some homeowners to purchase lower amounts of coverage or choose not to purchase flood insurance at all. Further, another stakeholder said higher flood insurance rates could affect property owners' home value and ability to sell their property. For example, one stakeholder said that potential buyers might decide not to purchase a home in a high-risk area after determining the cost of flood insurance for the property.

Stakeholders said that the political environment could prevent insurers from setting adequate rates. For example, they expressed concerns that efforts to increase flood insurance rates would likely face public resistance or be politically unpopular. Stakeholders said it was challenging for private insurers to gain enough confidence to enter the flood insurance market because they feared not being able to charge actuarially sound rates or obtain a reasonable rate of return. For example, stakeholders said that state by state approval of flood insurance rates might impede insurers' ability to obtain adequate rates. An insurer said that most state insurance regulators lacked knowledge about flood policies, but a state regulation official said that most states took a measured approach to rate regulation, with an eye toward allowing insurers to earn a reasonable profit. Further, one stakeholder said that private insurers would need flexibility to account for potential climate change effects when pricing flood, hurricane, and other risks associated with sea level rise. Although potential climate change effects would have a long time horizon, the stakeholder suggested it was an issue to consider regarding the regulatory environment for private insurers.

In addition, stakeholders said that private insurers would need freedom in underwriting policies so that they could accept and reject applicants as necessary to manage their risk portfolios. Insurable risks have certain characteristics that make providing coverage possible. As well as being estimable, for example, loss exposure should not be potentially catastrophic for the insurer.[34] Freedom to manage risk would help insurers manage potentially catastrophic losses and further encourage their participation in the flood insurance market. For example, insurers might determine that they needed to limit the number of policies in a geographic area because a single flood event could result in losses on many of those policies at the same time. Stakeholders said incentives would be needed to encourage insurers to assume greater risk, particularly in flood-prone areas. One stakeholder said the political environment could limit insurers' ability to accept and reject applicants as necessary to manage their risk exposure. Further, stakeholders said that different insurance regulations across states could further complicate insurers' ability to underwrite flood insurance.[35] One stakeholder said that insurers would need clarity on the political and regulatory environment before entering the flood market.

Adequate Consumer Participation Would Also Be Necessary

Insurers need to be able to manage their risk exposure by having a large, diverse risk pool with premiums at a level that property owners are willing and able to pay.[36] Having a large and diversified risk pool would enable an insurer to better estimate losses based on loss data it collected over time and to spread the losses over a large number of properties. Economically feasible premiums would provide an opportunity or incentive for property owners to obtain coverage. Further, in our prior work, one of the public policy goals we adapted for evaluating strategies for increasing private sector involvement in flood insurance was encouraging broad consumer participation in the flood insurance market. We previously have found that efforts to encourage broader participation in NFIP could reduce costs, depending on how they were implemented.[37] Likewise, a large risk pool could help private insurers manage their exposure.

Broad consumer participation in the market would also be necessary to address adverse selection—the phenomenon that occurs when only those most in need typically purchase insurance, creating a pool of only the highest-risk properties. In this case, insurers must be confident that homeowners other than those in the highest-risk areas will obtain flood insurance, because adverse selection can hamper an insurer's efforts to manage its risk. A 2006 study estimated that NFIP participation rates were as low as 50 percent in SFHAs, where property owners with loans from federally insured and regulated lenders were required to purchase flood insurance.[38] The study also found that participation rates outside of SFHAs were as low as 1 percent. Another study found that homeowners both within and outside SFHAs who did obtain flood insurance when purchasing their homes typically kept it for 2 to 4 years before canceling their policies.[39] Stakeholders said that homeowners were more likely to purchase flood insurance immediately following a flood event and to drop it later as their perception of their flood risk decreased.

Homeowners that do not purchase flood insurance, including many residing in SFHAs, make that decision for a number of reasons that would have to be addressed in order to make private flood insurance possible. Stakeholders said that affordability was one of the key challenges to providing flood insurance. In addition, stakeholders said that affordability could be a particularly difficult issue for low- and moderate-income homeowners, as evidenced by complaints surrounding rate increases under the Biggert-Waters Act. Further, stakeholders said that not all homeowners would be able to afford flood insurance at rates that private insurers would consider adequate for reflecting the full estimated risk of flood loss and allowing for profit.

Based on our analysis of stakeholder views and other information, many property owners may also have an inaccurate perception of their risk of flooding and thus do not buy flood insurance. For example, a 2012 study suggested that some property owners believe that only properties in SFHAs are in a flood zone and that properties located outside of SFHAs are not at risk of flooding.[40] Stakeholders said that it was difficult to convince homeowners to pay for coverage for an unlikely event, despite the potential for severe damage. The former definition of SFHAs as a "100-year" flood zone has contributed in part to this misperception, given the long time horizon, so that some property owners have assumed that after experiencing a flood loss, their properties would be free from flooding for the next 100 years.[41] And one stakeholder indicated that many consumers mistakenly assumed that their homeowners insurance policies included flood coverage. In addition, a banking association with whom we spoke said that some lending institutions did not see flood risk as a threat to their safety and soundness and therefore often did not require flood coverage at mortgage origination, potentially contributing further to homeowners' misperception of flood risk.

Finally, stakeholders suggested that many consumers did not obtain flood insurance because they assumed they would receive federal or state disaster assistance after a flood event. However, federal disaster assistance to individuals is limited. Disaster assistance is administered through several federal programs and is generally made available only after the President issues a disaster declaration, but homeowners seeking such assistance must first seek assistance from their flood insurance policy.[42] Further, while one federal grant program is available— the Individuals and Households Program—federal disaster assistance to individuals and businesses for the repair or replacement of structures consists primarily of federal loan programs. These include loans from the U.S. Small Business Administration that are available to all first-time applicants but to repeat applicants only if they have flood insurance. Homeowners can apply for up to $200,000 in home and property disaster loans for the repair or replacement of a primary residence to its predisaster condition. Business disaster loans of up to $2 million are the primary form of federal assistance for the repair and rebuilding of nonfarm, private sector disaster losses.[43] One stakeholder said many homeowners without flood insurance would not qualify for individual assistance or loans from the U.S. Small Business Administration and that homeowners might not have options—other than filing for bankruptcy—to recover financially from a flood event.[44] We previously reported that while the federal government has provided significant financial assistance after major disasters, the federal role is primarily to assist state and local governments, which have the central role in recovery efforts.[45]

Based on our analysis, all of these issues would need to be addressed to create the conditions that would encourage private insurers to consider providing flood insurance. Addressing them would be a complex task and would require difficult trade-offs. For example, raising rates beyond what FEMA currently charges could create significant hardship and put at risk the homes of those who could not afford flood insurance. Further, it could be a challenge to encourage property owners to purchase flood insurance, particularly when many of them do not believe they are exposed to the risk of flooding.

SEVERAL STRATEGIES COULD ENCOURAGE PRIVATE SECTOR INVOLVEMENT, BUT A GOVERNMENTAL ROLE WOULD LIKELY BE REQUIRED

Stakeholders with whom we spoke or who participated in our roundtable discussion identified several strategies that could be used to help transfer some of the responsibility of providing flood insurance from the federal government to the private sector. These strategies, or certain aspects of them, could be used jointly to promote the conditions that stakeholders said would be necessary for private sector involvement—the ability to assess risk, the freedom to charge adequate rates and manage risk, and adequate consumer participation. These strategies serve only as broad potential frameworks, and because of the complexity of providing flood insurance, the success of any reform effort would also depend on how it is structured and implemented. Further, stakeholders said that any strategy will likely require certain roles for federal, state, and local government entities.

Several Strategies Could Help Create Conditions for Private Sector Involvement

One strategy stakeholders identified, which we have also mentioned in previous reports, would be for Congress to eliminate subsidized rates, charge full-risk rates to all policyholders, and appropriate funding for a direct means-based subsidy to some policyholders.[46] A second strategy that stakeholders identified would be for the federal government to provide only residual insurance, serving as the insurer of last resort for properties that the private sector is unwilling to insure. Alternatively, a third strategy would be for the federal government to serve as a reinsurer and charge private insurers a premium for the federal government to assume risk for losses that exceed a predetermined amount. In addition to these strategies, stakeholders proposed others, including mandatory coverage, reinsurance for NFIP, and catastrophe bonds.

Full-Risk Rates with Targeted Subsidies

Stakeholders proposed eliminating all subsidized rates and charging all policyholders rates that reflected the full estimated risk of flooding, with Congress providing a direct means-based subsidy to some policyholders.[47] Stakeholders generally agreed that any subsidies should be explicit and provided directly to the policyholder instead of hidden in a discounted premium rate, partly because such hidden subsidies conceal a property's actual flood risk and encourage development in high-risk areas. While the premium levels may be sufficient to cover claims in years with lower losses, the subsidies result in insufficient premium revenue over the long term to cover years with higher losses. As a result, the cost of subsidies is disguised from taxpayers and evident only in FEMA's need to borrow from Treasury. Making the subsidies explicit would require Congress to appropriate funds for them, increasing transparency by showing the exact annual cost of the subsidies. Such subsidies could require determining eligibility requirements—for example, a means test—as well as the amount of subsidies. We suggested that Congress consider this approach in a previous report and this strategy continues to be an option that could offer benefits to the program and could be implemented independent of any increase in private sector involvement in flood insurance.[48]

Stakeholders said that removing the hidden subsidies and charging full-risk rates to all policyholders has a number of advantages. For example, demonstrating the political will to charge full-risk rates within NFIP could signal to private insurers a greater likelihood of being allowed the freedom to charge adequate rates in a private flood insurance market, thus encouraging their potential participation. However, stakeholders expressed concerns over discussions of proposals to delay rate increases, specifically those authorized by the Biggert-Waters Act.[49] These stakeholders said that such delays would increase private insurers' skepticism about the feasibility of participating in a private flood insurance market. Although raising rates could create affordability concerns for some, delaying the increases could reduce the chances of increasing private sector involvement in flood insurance, leaving taxpayers to continue paying for flood claims through future borrowing from Treasury.

Based on our analysis, providing means-tested subsidies to some property owners would allow Congress to address affordability concerns associated with premium rate increases. Currently, subsidies are available regardless of a property owner's ability to afford a full-risk premium. Means testing the subsidies would ensure that only those who could not afford full-risk rates would receive assistance and should increase the amount in premiums NFIP collects to cover losses. Collecting more in premiums by providing subsidies to fewer policyholders would reduce taxpayer costs, one of the goals for reforming catastrophe insurance. Finally, charging full-risk rates to all policyholders would demonstrate a property's actual flood risk to property owners, discourage further development in high-risk areas, and encourage property owners to invest in mitigation to lower their exposure to flood risk as well as their premium rate. However, while means-tested subsidies could make premium rates more affordable, they could also decrease a property owner's incentive to mitigate.

Stakeholders raised other concerns about increases in flood insurance premium rates. One stakeholder noted that rate increases could lower a home's market value because the cost of owning the home would rise. Further, stakeholders said that some communities with a high risk of flooding could become economically unviable if premium rate increases made flood insurance unaffordable for too many residents. For example, stakeholders as well as participants in congressional hearings have said that rate increases in some high-risk areas could make it unaffordable for many homeowners within a community to stay in their homes, which could lead to declining property values for homes and businesses. Premium rate increases could also cause some property owners to cancel their coverage or opt not to purchase it, particularly those who were not already mandated to purchase flood insurance.[50] Reduced participation could negate some of the benefits of providing the targeted subsidies. Means-based subsidies could soften some of these potential effects, but any solution will need to consider whether other steps would be necessary to limit adverse effects on particular communities.

Finally, the Biggert-Waters Act eliminates the transfer of subsidies when homes are sold and the renewal of subsidized policies if a policyholder deliberately chooses to allow flood coverage to lapse. We previously have reported that the continuing implementation of the act is expected to decrease the number of subsidized policies.[51] As the number of subsidized policies falls, NFIP's premium shortfall will decrease, helping its financial condition. Means-based subsidies could provide greater up- front savings by limiting the number of policyholders that would be eligible for the subsidies. However, there could be a point when the cost of continued means-based subsidies could exceed the level of subsidies that will otherwise exist as homes are sold or coverage lapses. Some stakeholders suggested that targeted subsidies should be temporary to help address this concern.

Government as Residual Insurer

According to stakeholders, another strategy for increasing the private sector's role in flood insurance is to have the federal government serve as the insurer of last resort. This strategy would give private insurers the opportunity to provide flood insurance to most property owners who desire it, and the federal government would offer coverage only to the highest-risk properties that private insurers were unwilling to underwrite. Stakeholders said that particularly in the early years, private insurers might be conservative regarding the properties they were willing to insure, but many might be willing to insure more properties as they grew comfortable with underwriting flood coverage. Some states have similarly structured residual insurance programs for other perils that could provide insight and offer lessons in structuring such a program for flood insurance.[52] For example, representatives from state residual insurance programs with whom we spoke said their programs charged rates that are higher than what would be available in the private market to ensure they remain insurers of last resort and discourage property owners from using it as an alternative to private sector coverage.

This strategy could help create the conditions we identified earlier in this report for increasing private sector involvement. To address private sector concerns about being able to accurately set rates, FEMA could grant private insurers access to historical claims data. However, as noted earlier FEMA would need to ensure that any disclosure complies with the Privacy Act. Further, the premium rates for residual coverage should be above what private market rates would be for comparable coverage to discourage property owners from using it as an alternative to private coverage.

Because this strategy would transfer many of NFIP's policies to the private sector, NFIP's total exposure would likely decrease. To the extent that the residual policies sold by NFIP were priced at full-risk rates, long- term taxpayer costs could be reduced. However, while full-risk rates would reduce taxpayer costs in the long-term, the average cost and volatility of the program's remaining policies would increase, because NFIP would be left with the highest-risk policies. Further, because these residual policies would have the highest risk, they would require high premium rates to cover their full risk of loss, potentially reducing consumer participation. Combining this option with means-based subsidies could help address affordability concerns and maintain consumer participation.

Government as Reinsurer

According to stakeholders, a third strategy for increasing private sector involvement in flood insurance would be for the federal government to provide reinsurance to private insurers.[53] Specifically, the federal government could provide a backstop for private insurers by agreeing to pay the difference when total claims exceeded a certain amount within a specified period. To fund reinsurance claims for catastrophic losses, the federal government could collect premiums from private insurers. Some stakeholders said that the private reinsurance industry might be able to provide some reinsurance to private insurers, reducing the federal government's potential role in reinsurance. However, other stakeholders expressed concerns that private reinsurers might raise premium rates or cancel coverage after a catastrophic loss year, creating uncertainty for private insurers that could affect their willingness to enter the flood insurance market.

Stakeholders said that the risk of insolvency in the event of catastrophic flood losses might make some private insurers hesitant to enter the flood insurance market and that providing reinsurance could help address these concerns and encourage their participation. If the federal government collected adequate reinsurance premiums, this strategy could also reduce costs to taxpayers, one of the goals for reforming natural catastrophe insurance, because most of the flood risk would be transferred to the private sector. However, the costs of these reinsurance premiums would likely be passed onto the policyholder, and the resulting higher rates could reduce consumer participation.

Once again, means- based subsidies could help soften these rate increases and maintain consumer participation.

Other Strategies

Stakeholders identified several other strategies that could help encourage private sector involvement in flood insurance.

Mandatory coverage. In particular, some stakeholders said that a federal mandate could help achieve the level of consumer participation necessary to make the private sector comfortable with providing flood insurance coverage. For example, some stakeholders said that the federal government could mandate that homeowners insurance policies include flood coverage or that all homeowners purchase flood insurance.[54]

Either mandate could increase the number of homeowners purchasing flood insurance, something that could help private insurers diversify and manage the risk of their flood insurance portfolio and address concerns about adverse selection. However, the stakeholders were also concerned that private companies might oppose a mandate that homeowners policies include flood coverage, potentially raising legal issues. Further, stakeholders said that some property owners— particularly those who perceived their flood risk to be low—might also resist being required to purchase flood insurance. Finally, as we have reported the federal government has faced challenges with enforcing the current mandatory purchase requirement for flood insurance, which applies to properties in high-risk areas with federally regulated mortgages.[55] If the federal government faces similar challenges with additional mandates, it might not realize the intended benefits of increased consumer participation.

Reinsure NFIP. Other stakeholders discussed NFIP purchasing reinsurance from the private sector to cover exposure to catastrophic losses rather than relying on borrowing from Treasury.[56] While doing so would increase private sector involvement in flood insurance, the federal government would still play an active role in flood insurance, because NFIP would still serve as the main provider of primary flood insurance coverage. However, the federal government's exposure to catastrophic losses could be reduced. On the other hand, stakeholders noted that private companies might cancel reinsurance after a catastrophic loss year, leading to uncertainty as to the degree to which the federal government's exposure would be mitigated. Further, stakeholders said that NFIP may need to collect additional premiums on its existing policies to pay for the reinsurance. However, given that NFIP's current premium levels are insufficient, NFIP may be unable to pay for this additional expense.

Catastrophe bonds. Stakeholders said that as an alternative to reinsurance, NFIP might be able to limit its exposure to large losses by transferring risk to capital markets through insurance-linked securities such as catastrophe bonds. For example, NFIP could issue interest- bearing bonds to investors willing to bear the risk of losing some of their investment if flood claims exceeded a predetermined amount.

Like reinsurance, catastrophe bonds could help NFIP manage its risk exposure, but again it would need to be able to collect adequate premiums to cover any necessary payments of principal or interest. We have previously reported that state insurance entities, as well as private sector insurers, have used catastrophe bonds to manage their risk.[57]

A Governmental Role Would Remain Even in a Private Flood Insurance Market

Stakeholders with whom we spoke or who participated in our roundtable discussion said that no matter which strategies Congress might choose for increasing private sector involvement in flood insurance, the federal government would likely still have some role. For example, some strategies include transforming the federal government's role from primary provider of flood insurance to a residual insurer or a reinsurer. As the private sector increases its role in providing flood coverage, various government entities could collaborate on other important roles. In particular, stakeholders said that it would continue to be important for federal, state, and local governments to encourage mitigation through direct funding or other less costly strategies and to promote risk awareness among consumers. Stakeholders said that government entities want to reduce property owners' current and future exposure to flood risk and increase the resiliency of their structures. Stakeholders also said that with private flood insurance, both the insurance company and the policyholder would have some incentive to mitigate, the insurer to reduce its risk exposure and the policyholder to lower the premium rate. More generally, stakeholders also said that various government entities should continue developing and enforcing building codes and land use agreements in order to reduce the flood risk of current structures and prevent future development in high-risk areas. Stakeholders also said that the federal government should ensure consistent insurance standards and regulations across states, in part through streamlined state regulations or federal oversight, to allow insurers to charge adequate rates.

CONCLUSION

While a number of conditions are important to attract private sector participation in the flood insurance market, key among them is the ability to charge rates that fully reflect the estimated risk of flooding. The Biggert-Waters Act includes a number of provisions that begin moving NFIP toward full-risk rates for some properties, a critical first step. Delaying or repealing rate increases in the Biggert-Waters Act may address affordability concerns but would likely continue to increase NFIP's long-term burden on taxpayers. Further, it may reinforce private insurers' skepticism that they would ever be permitted to charge adequate rates and make their participation unlikely in the foreseeable future. As debates over the private sector's role continue, one step to address the burden on low- and moderate-income policyholders could be taken immediately. As we have suggested previously, Congress could eliminate subsidized rates, charge full-risk rates to all policyholders, and appropriate funds for a direct means-based subsidy to eligible policyholders. The movement to full-risk rates would encourage private sector participation, and the explicit subsidy would address affordability concerns, raise awareness of the risks associated with living in harm's way, and decrease costs to taxpayers, depending on the extent and amount of the subsidy.

AGENCY COMMENTS

We provided a draft of this report to the Federal Emergency Management Agency (FEMA) and the Federal Insurance Office for their review and comment. FEMA provided technical comments, which we have incorporated into the report.

Alicia Puente Cackley
Director, Financial Markets and Community Investment

APPENDIX I: OBJECTIVES, SCOPE, AND METHODOLOGY

The Biggert-Waters Flood Insurance Reform Act of 2012 (Biggert-Waters Act) mandated that GAO conduct a number of studies, including this study on assessing a broad range of options, methods, and strategies for privatizing the National Flood Insurance Program (NFIP).[58] This report discusses (1) conditions needed for private sector involvement in flood insurance and (2) strategies for increasing it.

To both identify conditions needed for private sector involvement in flood insurance and evaluate the benefits and challenges of strategies for increasing private sector involvement, we reviewed the laws, regulations, and history of NFIP, Federal Emergency Management Agency (FEMA) reports, academic studies, our prior work on NFIP, and other documentation and reports. We also held a roundtable in August 2013 composed of a variety of stakeholders to obtain their views on these issues. The 14 stakeholders participating in the roundtable included FEMA officials; state insurance regulators; a catastrophe modeling firm; an academic; and individuals representing associations of private insurers, reinsurers, actuaries, consumers, and floodplain managers. We supplemented information obtained through the roundtable with interviews with stakeholders representing the groups listed above as well as Federal Insurance

Office officials; state residual insurance programs; and groups representing insurance adjusters, insurance agents, realtors, and mortgage bankers.

We selected a diverse group of stakeholders for the roundtable and interviews based on type of organization, role, and membership. In addition, we identified some stakeholders based on work conducted from a prior report, and suggestions from other stakeholders. The roundtable discussion focused on four broad themes that included:

- a policy goals framework for evaluating options for increasing private sector involvement in flood insurance,
- barriers to private sector involvement that would need to be overcome,
- options for private sector involvement and associated benefits and challenges, and
- the governmental role that would remain in a private flood insurance market.

We identified four public policy goals to evaluate options for changing the federal role in natural catastrophe insurance in a prior report.[59] These goals are generally consistent with the evaluation criteria the stakeholders discussed. Roundtable participants and other stakeholders generally agreed that these goals were applicable for evaluating options for increasing private sector involvement in flood insurance.

We conducted this performance audit from March 2013 to January 2014 in accordance with generally accepted government auditing standards. Those standards require that we plan and perform the audit to obtain sufficient, appropriate evidence to provide a reasonable basis for our findings and conclusions based on our audit objectives. We believe that the evidence obtained provides a reasonable basis for our findings and conclusions based on our audit objectives.

End Notes

[1] FEMA has authority to borrow money from Treasury to pay losses that exceed premium revenue and any accumulated surplus. Treasury charges FEMA interest on the outstanding debt. Before Superstorm Sandy, this borrowing authority stood at $20.725 billion. In January 2013, Congress passed and the President signed into law a $9.7 billion increase in this authority to pay flood claims related to Superstorm Sandy, raising FEMA's borrowing authority to a total of $30.425 billion. Pub. L. No. 113-1, § 1(a), 127 Stat. 3, 3 (2013).

[2] The Biggert-Waters Flood Insurance Reform Act of 2012 mandates that FEMA develop a plan for repaying its debt to Treasury. Pub. L. No. 112-141, Div. F, Tit. II, Subtit. A, § 100213(a), 126 Stat. 405, 923 (codified at 42 U.S.C. § 4016(c)).

[3] See GAO, *High-Risk Program*, GAO-06-497T (Washington, D.C.: Mar. 15, 2006); and *High-Risk Series: An Update*, GAO-13-359T (Washington, D.C.: Feb. 13, 2013).

[4] Pub. L. No. 90-448, Tit. XIII, 82 Stat. 476, 572 (1968).

[5] These properties generally have higher loss rates than unsubsidized properties. In 2008, we reported that subsidized properties accounted for the majority of repetitive loss properties—properties that have experienced multiple flood losses—and made up around 1 percent of the total policies but 30 percent of the claims dollars paid. See GAO, *Flood Insurance: Options for Addressing the Financial Impact of Subsidized Premium Rates on the National Flood Insurance Program*, GAO-09-20 (Washington, D.C.: Nov. 14, 2008).

[6] Pub. L. No. 112-141, Div. F, Tit. II, Subtit. A, 126 Stat. 405, 916 (2012). Prior to the Biggert-Waters Act, FEMA could "grandfather" properties that were already in the program when new flood maps placed them in higher-risk zones, allowing some property owners to pay premium rates that applied to the previous lower-risk zone.

[7] Pub. L. No. 112-141, § 100232(a).

[8] See GAO, *Flood Insurance: Implications of Changing Coverage Limits and Expanding Coverage*, GAO-13-568 (Washington, D.C.: July 3, 2013).

[9] To be eligible for these discounts, communities must participate in the Community Rating System, a voluntary program established in 1990 to encourage community floodplain management activities that exceed the minimum NFIP standards. Under the Community Rating System, flood insurance premium rates are discounted to reward community actions that meet three goals: (1) reduce flood damage to insurable property, (2) strengthen and support the insurance aspects of NFIP, and (3) encourage a comprehensive approach to floodplain management.

[10] Not all participating NFIP communities have residents or businesses with policies.

[11] The Bunning-Bereuter-Blumenauer Flood Insurance Reform Act of 2004 amended the existing definition of the term "repetitive loss structure" to the current one—a structure covered by a contract for flood insurance that (a) has incurred flood-related damage on two occasions resulting in repair costs that, on average, equaled or exceeded 25 percent of the structure's value, and (b) at the time of the second incidence, the contract for flood insurance must contain increased cost of compliance coverage. 42 U.S.C. § 4121(a)(7).

[12] 49 Stat. 1570 (1936).

[13] Federal Emergency Management Agency, *National Flood Insurance Program: Program Description* (Washington, D.C.: Aug. 1, 2002).

[14] Pub. L. No. 89-339, 79 Stat. 1301 (1965).

[15] Pub. L. No. 89-339, § 5 (mandating feasibility study); National Flood Insurance Act of 1968, Pub. L. No. 90-448, Title XIII, 82 Stat. 476, 572.

[16] GAO, *Economic Development: HUD's Determination to Convert from Industry to Government Operation of the National Flood Insurance Program*, CED-78-122 (Washington, D.C.: May 31, 1978).

[17] Pub. L. No. 93-234, 87 Stat. 975 (1973).

[18] Pub. L. No. 103-325, Tit. V, 108 Stat. 2160, 2255 (1994).

[19] Pub. L. No. 108-264, Tit. I, § 102, 118 Stat. 712, 714 (2004). According to FEMA, the key mitigation steps for residential properties are elevating a building to or above the area's base flood elevation, relocating the building to an area with lower flood risk, or demolishing the building and turning the property into green space. A community can also take steps to reduce flood risk to an area by diverting the flow of water through well- designed channels and retaining walls or by containing the water through ponds and green space.

[20] Pub. L. No. 112-141, §§ 100203, 100205. For single-family properties, severe repetitive loss properties are those that have incurred at least four NFIP claims payments exceeding $5,000 each, with the cumulative amount of such claims payments exceeding $20,000; or at least two separate claims payments with a cumulative total that exceeds the property's value. For multifamily properties, FEMA will define the term by regulation.

[21] Pub. L. No. 112-141, § 100205(c)(3) (codified at 42 U.S.C. § 4015(e)(2)).

[22] Pub. L. No. 112-141, § 100205(a)(1)(B) (codified at 42 U.S.C. § 4014(g)(3)-(4)).

[23] Pub. L. No. 112-141, § 100205(a)(1)(B) (codified at 42 U.S.C. § 4014(g)(1)-(2)).

[24] Subject to any other statutory provision in 42 U.S.C. ch. 50. Pub. L. No. 112-141, § 100207 (codified at 42 U.S.C. § 4015(h)).

[25] *See, e.g.*, Homeowner Flood Insurance Affordability Act of 2013, S. 1610, 113th Cong. (2013); Homeowner Flood Insurance Affordability Act of 2013, H.R. 3370, 113th Cong. (2013); a bill to improve the National Flood Insurance Program, and for other purposes, S. 996, 113th Cong. (2013); Flood Insurance Premium Relief Act of 2013, H.R. 1267, 113th Cong. (2013); and Flood Victim Premium Relief Act of 2013, H.R. 960, 113th Cong. (2013).

[26] See GAO, *Natural Disasters: Public Policy Options for Changing the Federal Role in Natural Catastrophe Insurance*, GAO-08-7 (Washington, D.C.: Nov. 26, 2007).

[27] We obtained views from stakeholders through a roundtable discussion as well as individual interviews. References to stakeholders throughout this report refer to information obtained either through our roundtable discussion, individual interviews, or both. Further, information attributed to stakeholders does not imply an agreement among all stakeholders with whom we spoke, but instead indicates something mentioned by multiple stakeholders.

[28] George E. Rejda, *Principles of Risk Management and Insurance,* 8th ed. (Boston, Mass.: Pearson Education, Inc, 2003).

[29] Federal Emergency Management Agency, *National Flood Insurance Program: Program Description* (Washington, D.C.: Aug. 1, 2002).

[30] Modeling companies determine the probability of flooding and the associated cost of damage based on an analysis of flood hazards and a building's exposure and vulnerability to those hazards.

[31] The Biggert-Waters Act requires the newly created Technical Mapping Advisory Council to develop recommendations for FEMA for future conditions mapping, including the best available methodology to consider the impact of the rise in the sea level and future development on flood risk, and present its recommendations in a report. FEMA is required to implement such future risk assessment recommendations. Pub. L. No. 112-141, § 100215(d).

[32] Pub. L. No. 93-579, 88 Stat. 1896 (1974) (codified, as amended, at 5 U.S.C. § 552a).

[33] We previously reported that charging full-risk rates would improve NFIP's financial soundness but could reduce property owner participation. See GAO, *Flood Insurance: Public Policy Goals Provide a Framework for Reform*, GAO-11-670T (Washington, D.C.: June 23, 2011).

[34] Rejda, *Principles of Risk Management and Insurance.*

[35] States, rather than federal government, primarily regulate insurance. See GAO, *Insurance Markets: Impacts of and Regulatory Response to the 2007-2009 Financial Crisis*, GAO-13-583 (Washington, D.C.: June 27, 2013).

[36] Rejda, *Principles of Risk Management and Insurance.*

[37] GAO-11-670T.

[38] RAND Corporation, *The National Flood Insurance Program's Market Penetration Rate: Estimates and Policy Implications* (Santa Monica, Ca.: American Institutes for Research, Feb. 2006).

[39] Erwann Michel-Kerjan, Sabine Lemoyne de Forges, and Howard Kunreuther, "Policy Tenure under the U.S. National Flood Insurance Program (NFIP)," *Risk Analysis*, vol. 32, no. 4, (2012).

[40] Michel-Kerjan, Lemoyne de Forges, and Kunreuther, "Policy Tenure under NFIP," 10-12.

[41] To clarify the perception of risk among homeowners, FEMA revised the definition of SFHA to land "subject to a 1 percent or greater chance of flooding in any given year."

[42] GAO, *Disaster Assistance: Federal Assistance for Permanent Housing Primarily Benefited Homeowners; Opportunities Exist to Better Target Rental Housing Needs*, GAO-10-17 (Washington, D.C.: Jan. 14, 2010).

[43] Homeowners may also purchase mortgage insurance through the Mortgage Insurance for Disaster Victims Section 203(h) program, administered by HUD, to finance the purchase or reconstruction of homes in presidentially designated disaster areas.

[44] Other types of federal assistance might be available to qualifying disaster victims through programs not specific to disasters. For example, the U.S. Department of Agriculture's Rural Housing Repair Loan and Grant program provides loans of up to $20,000 and grants of up to $7,500 to very-low-income homeowners to repair, improve, or modernize their dwellings, or remove health and safety hazards, in eligible rural areas. Further, individuals or households with very low, low, and moderate incomes can obtain loans through the U.S. Department of Agriculture's Section 502 program to build, repair, renovate, or relocate a home in an eligible rural area.

[45] For example, FEMA's Hazard Mitigation Grant Program provides assistance to states, local governments, and Indian tribes to implement long-term hazard mitigation measures following a major disaster, and the agency's Flood Mitigation Assistance Program provides funds to assist states, local governments, and Indian tribes in implementing measures that reduce or eliminate the long-term risk of flood damage to buildings, manufactured homes, and other structures insured under NFIP. In addition, HUD has provided funding to states through the Community Development Block Grant program. States have often relied on this program for flexible funding that can be applied to disasters to help rebuild communities and, in some cases, make funds or services available to residents. See GAO-10-17.

[46] See GAO-09-20 and GAO, *FEMA: Action Needed to Improve Administration of the National Flood Insurance Program*, GAO-11-297 (Washington, D.C., June 9, 2011).

[47] Congress could provide such a subsidy in a number of ways including vouchers or tax rebates.

[48] See GAO-11-297.

[49] As we have discussed, the Biggert-Waters Act eliminates subsidies in a number of situations, including for nonprimary residences, severe repetitive loss properties, business properties, properties that are sold, and when insurance coverage lapses.

[50] Regulated lending institutions shall not make, increase, extend, or renew any designated loan unless the building or mobile home and any personal property securing the loan is covered by flood insurance for the term of the loan. 42 U.S.C. § 4012a.

[51] See GAO, *Flood Insurance: More Information Needed on Subsidized Properties*, GAO-13-607 (Washington, D.C.: July 3, 2013).

[52] See GAO, *Natural Catastrophe Insurance Coverage Remains a Challenge for State Programs*, GAO-10-568R (Washington, D.C., May 17, 2010).

[53] Reinsurance is insurance for insurers that enables the insurer to transfer some of its risk to another insurer, called a reinsurer.

[54] In a separate report, we are examining perils that are excluded from homeowners insurance policies.

[55] See GAO, *Federal Emergency Management Agency: Ongoing Challenges Facing the National Flood Insurance Program*, GAO-08-118T (Washington, D.C.: Oct. 2, 2007).

[56] The Biggert-Waters Act allows for NFIP to secure private market reinsurance, so FEMA would have the authority to do this without additional congressional action. Pub. L. No. 112-141, § 100232(d).

[57] See GAO-10-568R.

[58] Pub. L. No. 112-141, § 100232(a).

[59] See GAO, *Natural Disasters: Public Policy Options for Changing the Federal Role in Natural Catastrophe Insurance*, GAO-08-7 (Washington, D.C.: Nov. 26, 2007).

In: Flood and Homeowners Insurance
Editor: Ella Grace Irwin

ISBN: 978-1-63117-888-7

Chapter 2

HOMEOWNERS INSURANCE: MULTIPLE CHALLENGES MAKE EXPANDING PRIVATE COVERAGE DIFFICULT*

United States Government Accountability Office

WHY GAO DID THIS STUDY

Homeowners insurance protects against a range of perils, but policies do not insure against all risks. Owners whose homes are damaged by natural and other disasters not covered by their insurance can be exposed to serious financial losses. Federal and state initiatives provide some assistance for catastrophes, which can involve significant taxpayer expense. With coastal populations growing and the possibility of more frequent and severe weather, more homeowners could experience heavy losses not covered by homeowners insurance, putting increasing financial pressure on government programs and thus on taxpayers.

GAO was asked to study the possibility of private insurers providing more comprehensive insurance. This report addresses (1) what perils homeowners policies typically cover and exclude, (2) how exclusions impact homeowners and taxpayers and the potential benefits of more comprehensive coverage, and (3) what additional perils insurers might be willing to cover and what

---

* This is an edited, reformatted and augmented version of the United States Government Accountability Office publication, GAO-14-179, dated January 2014.

challenges are associated with expanding policies. GAO reviewed homeowners insurance policies and conducted interviews with the National Association of Insurance Commissioners, other industry organizations, consumer advocates, and risk experts, among others.

GAO requested comments on a draft of this report from the Federal Insurance Office and the National Association of Insurance Commissioners. Both provided technical comments which we incorporated into the report as appropriate.

WHAT GAO FOUND

Homeowners insurance policies typically protect homes, garages and other structures, and personal belongings from damage caused by perils such as fire, hail, lightning, explosion, and theft, among others. The insurance industry considers these perils insurable because they are accidental, predictable, and do not involve catastrophic losses. These policies also typically exclude losses from a number of perils, including disasters caused by floods, earthquakes, and war. Industry officials said that such events are difficult to predict and involve extensive losses that are a challenge for private insurers to cover. Insurers also exclude losses from defective products, which industry participants said could be addressed by manufacturer warranties and commercial general liability insurance. Intentional losses; damage from wear, tear, or neglect; and losses caused simultaneously by covered and uncovered perils, such as wind (covered) and flood (uncovered) during a hurricane are also generally excluded.

Policy exclusions can impact homeowners, communities, and state and federal governments. When excluded losses occur, they can create significant costs for homeowners to repair homes and replace possessions. Wide-scale catastrophes can also cause shortages of building materials and contractors that delay reconstruction and substantially increase the costs of repairing homes. When damage to properties caused by excluded losses is not repaired, affected communities may experience blight and face reduced tax revenue. When federal and state governments have stepped in to cover what private insurers exclude, taxpayers may face a significant expense. In addition to federal disaster assistance, the National Flood Insurance Program (NFIP) paid more than $7 billion in claims after Superstorm Sandy. In Florida, insurers and policyholders can be assessed extra charges to help pay for state efforts to cover wind damage where it is not covered by insurers. Industry participants suggested that expanded private coverage could provide additional protection for homeowners and reduce reliance on government programs, but the resulting policy premiums would likely be prohibitively expensive for many homeowners.

Multiple factors make expanding private coverage challenging and several conditions would need to be addressed for insurers to offer more comprehensive insurance. A main challenge is that expanded coverage would have higher costs, potentially limiting consumer demand. Even if insurers charged higher rates that were based on risk, the severity and unpredictability of catastrophic losses could still jeopardize insurers' solvency. Some industry participants said that insurers and others are discussing possibilities for expanding private homeowners coverage, with a focus on risk-based premiums, mitigation efforts, effective building codes, and sound land use policies. The challenging mix of financial risk, political and regulatory issues, policy cost, and consumer demand has thus far prevented private sector insurers in the U.S. from offering flood insurance to homeowners, let alone more comprehensive or all-perils policies. Because of this mix of factors, some in the insurance industry have suggested that a continuing financial role by federal and possibly state governments may be required, and that ensuring a response to the impact of disasters and other perils will require the cooperation and resources of government, homeowners, and insurers, as well as balance in the assumption of risk and cost by each of these parties.

ABBREVIATIONS

CEA	California Earthquake Authority
FAIR	Fair Access to Insurance Requirements
FEMA	Federal Emergency Management Agency
FHCF	Florida Hurricane Catastrophe Fund
FWUA	Florida Windstorm Underwriting Association
IHP	Individuals and Households Program
III	Insurance Information Institute
ISO	Insurance Services Office
JUA	Florida Residential Property and Casualty Joint Underwriting Association
NAIC	National Association of Insurance Commissioners
NFIP	National Flood Insurance Program

January 30, 2014

Congressional Requesters

Homeowners in the United States are exposed to a wide range of disasters, including hurricanes, earthquakes, floods, and wildfires, and may also experience losses from lightning, hail, and fire, among other perils.[1] When these and other catastrophes occur, they not only devastate individuals and communities by destroying homes and other possessions, but also have a significant financial impact on homeowners, insurers, and state and federal governments. Superstorm Sandy, for example, caused over $18 billion in privately insured property losses, according to industry estimates, and the Federal Emergency Management Agency (FEMA) has paid more than $7 billion in claims through the National Flood Insurance Program (NFIP).

At the same time, the population of coastal states facing possible weather risks such as floods and hurricanes is growing. As of 2010, approximately 39 percent of the nation's total population, approximately 123 million people, lived in coastal counties, a 39 percent increase since 1970.[2] As of 2012, properties in hurricane-prone areas on the coast had an insured value of about $15 trillion, with Florida, New York, and Texas having the greatest risk exposure. In addition to floods and hurricanes, some states such as California face risks such as earthquakes and wildfires while Florida faces risks from sinkholes. With more people moving to coastal areas, the possibility of more frequent and severe weather could impact the ability of homeowners and insurers to protect homes and other property. These and other risks underscore the importance of insurance to help protect homes and property from various hazards. Homeowners insurance, however, does not cover all types of perils and some homeowners may not clearly understand what protection their policy includes and excludes until after an event occurs. Homeowners count on insurance to help rebuild their lives and minimize financial burdens and may suffer severe losses depending on the type of peril and the coverage offered in their policies.

In light of recent concerns about homeowners' ability to protect their assets, GAO was asked to examine issues associated with the possibility of more comprehensive homeowners insurance. This report addresses (1) the perils homeowners policies typically cover and exclude; (2) the impact of exclusions on homeowners, communities, and taxpayers and the potential benefits of more comprehensive coverage; and (3) the additional perils insurers might be willing to cover and the challenges associated with offering expanded coverage. To do this work, we reviewed a standard homeowners policy from the insurance industry and policies from select property/casualty insurers that were chosen by market share based on premiums written and participation in different geographic markets. We also interviewed insurance industry association officials, consumer advocates, and academic experts. Further, we interviewed selected state insurance regulators from states that experience major perils such as floods, hurricanes, and earthquakes, among others.[3] Finally, we obtained information from a panel of insurance experts who participated in a roundtable discussion on issues associated with private insurers' willingness and ability to cover floods and other natural catastrophes. We discuss our scope and methodology in more detail in appendix I.

We conducted this performance audit from December 2012 to January 2014 in accordance with generally accepted government auditing standards. Those standards require that we plan and perform the audit to obtain sufficient, appropriate evidence to provide a reasonable basis for our findings and conclusions based on our audit objectives. We believe that the evidence obtained provides a reasonable basis for our findings and conclusions based on our audit objectives.

BACKGROUND

Homeowners Insurance Policies

Homeowners insurance provides consumers with financial protection against unexpected losses. Most homeowners policies provide a package of coverage that protects against damage to different types of property and liability for injuries and property damage policyholders cause to others. The following are the main types of coverage:

- *Dwelling.* Pays for damage to a house and to attached structures, including plumbing, electrical wiring, heating, and permanently installed air-conditioning systems.
- *Other structures.* Pays for damage to fences, tool sheds, freestanding garages, guest cottages, and other structures not attached to the dwelling.
- *Personal property.* Pays for the value of personal possessions, including furniture, electronics, appliances, and clothing damaged or

lost even when they are not on the subject property—for instance, when they are in an off-site storage locker or with a child at college.

- *Loss of use.* Pays some additional living expenses while a home is being repaired.[4]
- *Personal liability.* Pays for financial loss from lawsuits for injuries or damages to someone else.
- *Medical payments.* Pays medical bills for people hurt on the property or by a pet.[5]

Homeowners can purchase several types of insurance policies. These policies differ based on the perils they cover (see table 1). For example, named perils policies insure against losses caused by perils that are specifically listed in the policies. Open peril policies are broader policies that insure against losses caused by all perils, except those that are specifically excluded. However, according to industry participants with whom we spoke, currently no homeowners policies are available that cover every possible peril a homeowner could face.

Table 1. Types of Homeowners Insurance Policies for Single-Family Homes

Policy type	Description of policy
HO-2: Broad Policy	A named peril policy, it covers the dwelling and personal property against 16 perils listed in the policy.
HO-3: Special Policy	The most commonly written policy, it is a combination of a named peril policy and an open peril policy. It covers the dwelling against all perils except those specifically excluded (such as flood and earthquake) and covers personal property against 16 named perils.
HO-5: Comprehensive Policy	More comprehensive than the HO-3, it is an open peril policy that covers the dwelling and personal property against all perils, except those that are specifically excluded (such as flood and earthquake).
HO-8: Modified Coverage Policy	A named peril policy, it is designed for older homes, where the cost to replace is greater than the market value.

Source: Insurance Services Office (ISO), National Association of Insurance Commissioners, and Insurance Information Institute.

Note: These policy types are examples of homeowners insurance policies developed by the ISO, which is a provider of data and analytics for the risk management industry, including property/casualty insurers. ISO has developed other policy types not included in this table, as have other companies.

In addition to different policy types, homeowners may choose between three different levels of coverage for their homeowners policies.[6] These options are:

- *Actual cash value*. This type of coverage pays to replace the home or possessions after deducting for depreciation. Value is determined by taking into consideration the age of the home and wear and tear.[7] This level of coverage may not be enough to fully repair or replace the damage.
- *Replacement cost*. This type of coverage pays the cost of rebuilding or repairing the home or replacing possessions, up to the coverage limit, without a deduction for depreciation. It allows for the repair or rebuilding of the home by using materials of similar kind and quality.
- *Guaranteed (or extended) replacement cost*. This option is the most comprehensive and expensive. It pays a certain percentage, typically 20 to 25 percent, over the coverage limit to rebuild the home in the event that materials and labor costs increase as a result of a widespread disaster.[8]

The HO-2, HO-3, and HO-5 policies typically provide replacement cost coverage on the structures.[9] Contents coverage under homeowner policies is typically provided on an actual cash value basis, unless the replacement cost option is purchased. The HO-8 typically provides coverage for older homes on an actual cash value basis. Full replacement cost policies may not be available for some older homes.

Cost of Insurance to Homeowners

Several factors affect the premiums consumers pay for their homeowners policies, including the type and characteristics of the home. For example, homes that are primarily brick or masonry typically have lower premiums than wood frame homes, and older homes and homes in poor condition tend to have higher premiums than newer homes and homes in good condition. A homeowner's characteristics, such as a history of filing claims, and choices, such as the dollar amount of coverage selected, may also impact the premium cost. Other factors that impact the premium cost include the degree of exposure to catastrophes (such as hurricanes or earthquakes), the type of protection devices in the home (such as sprinkler or security systems), and the type of structures on the property (such as swimming pools or trampolines).

In addition to paying premiums for their insurance policies, homeowners generally have to pay a deductible when they file a claim—that is, an amount of money a policyholder must pay before an insurance policy will pay for a loss. The deductible applies to both home and personal property coverage and is paid on each claim. Higher deductibles generally mean lower policy premiums. In some locations, there are also catastrophe deductibles that a homeowner must pay when a major natural disaster occurs. They are expressed as a percentage of a claim instead of an insured amount.

State Regulation of Insurance

Insurance in the United States is primarily regulated at the state level.[10] State insurance regulators are responsible for enforcing state insurance laws and regulations, including through the licensing of agents, the review of insurance products and premium rates, and the examination of insurers' financial solvency and market conduct. The insurance regulators of the 50 states, the District of Columbia, and the U.S. territories created and govern the National Association of Insurance Commissioners (NAIC), which is the standard-setting and regulatory support organization for the U.S. insurance industry. Through the NAIC, state insurance regulators establish standards and best practices, conduct peer review, and coordinate their regulatory oversight. NAIC staff supports these efforts and represents the collective views of state regulators domestically and internationally. NAIC members, together with the central resources of the NAIC, form the national system of state-based regulation in the United States.

Risk Management by Insurers

Insurers assume some financial risk when writing policies, but also employ various strategies to manage risk so they can earn profits, limit potential financial exposures, and build the capital needed to pay claims. For example, insurance companies establish underwriting standards, such as refusing to insure customers who pose unacceptable levels of risk, or limiting coverage in particular geographic areas. Insurance companies may also purchase reinsurance, or insurance for insurance companies, to cover specific portions of their financial risk. For catastrophic losses, insurers may also sell financial instruments such as catastrophe bonds. Reinsurers use similar strategies to manage their risks.

Both insurers and reinsurers must also predict the frequency and severity of insured losses with some reliability to best manage financial risk. In some cases, these events can be fairly predictable. For example, the incidence of most automobile claims is predictable, and losses generally do not occur to large numbers of policyholders at the same time. However, some infrequent events, such as hurricanes, are so severe that they pose unique challenges for insurers and reinsurers. The unpredictability and sheer size of these types of events can result in substantial losses that deplete insurers' and reinsurers' capital. If a company believes that the risk of loss is unacceptably high given the rate that can be charged, it may decide not to offer coverage.

Government Involvement in Homeowners Insurance

If the private sector will not insure a particular type of risk, the public sector may create markets to ensure the availability of insurance. For example, several states have established Fair Access to Insurance Requirements (FAIR) plans, which pool resources from insurers doing business in the state to make property insurance available to property owners who cannot obtain coverage in the private insurance market, or cannot do so at an affordable rate. In addition, some states have established windstorm insurance pools that pool resources from private insurers to make insurance for wind risks available to property owners who cannot obtain it in the private insurance market.[11]

At the federal level, Congress established NFIP in 1968 to provide flood coverage to homeowners where voluntary markets do not readily exist.[12] FEMA is responsible for the oversight and management of NFIP.[13] Designed to help reduce the cost of federal assistance after floods, NFIP may be the sole source of insurance to some residents of flood-prone areas. Participating communities are required to adopt and enforce floodplain management regulations, thereby reducing the risks of flooding and the costs of repairing flood damage. Under the program, the federal government assumes the liability for covered losses and sets premium rates and coverage limitations. Like private insurance companies, federal and state government insurance programs also collect premiums, but their rates do not always reflect the risks that the programs assume, in part because they are designed to keep insurance affordable for most homeowners.[14]

POLICIES COVER AND EXCLUDE VARIOUS PERILS BASED ON POLICY PROVISIONS AND OTHER FACTORS

Homeowners policies provide protections against a number of perils that can impact individuals and families. Policies, however, do not protect against all perils that homeowners could face. Various sections of a homeowners insurance policy outline perils covered and those the policy excludes. Policy provisions and other factors, such as location, can impact the coverage insurers offer homeowners.

Homeowners Policies Typically Cover a Range of Perils

Homeowners insurance policies typically cover a range of perils and are critical to providing financial protection against losses such as fire and theft, among others. According to many industry participants, the Insurance Services Office's (ISO) HO-3 policy is the most commonly purchased homeowners policy and outlines the typical coverage and exclusions found in most homeowners policies.[15] The HO-3 covers a person's dwelling or home and other structures—such as detached garage, or shed—against all perils except those specifically excluded. This is commonly known as "open perils" coverage. For possessions, or personal property, the HO-3 covers only those perils listed in the policy, typically the 16 outlined below in table 2. Insurers refer to this kind of coverage as "named peril" coverage.

Private insurers determine which perils are insurable risks on the basis of certain characteristics or criteria of the losses associated with them, including the following:[16]

- *Losses that are definite and measurable.* The loss should be definite or determinate in time, place, and cause, and the insurer must be capable of setting a dollar value on the amount of the loss.
- *Losses that are sudden, random, and accidental.* The loss must result from chance and not be something that is certain to happen. If a future loss were sure to occur, coverage would have to be priced at the full value of the loss plus an additional amount for the expenses incurred.
- *Losses that are not catastrophic.* The losses should not affect a very large percentage of an insurance company's policyholders at the same time in, for example, a limited geographic area.[17] The losses should be

independent of each other in order to spread and minimize risk. Additionally, the peril should not be so catastrophic that the insurer would be unable to charge a sufficient premium to cover the exposure.

- *Losses for which the law of large numbers applies.* There must be a sufficiently large number of homogeneous units exposed to random losses, both historically and prospectively, to make the future losses reasonably predictable. This principle works best when there are many losses with similar characteristics spread across a large group. The greater the experience with losses, the better insurers can estimate both the frequency and severity of future losses.

Table 2. Perils Covered for Personal Property in the HO-3

1.	Fire or lightning
2.	Windstorm or hail[a]
3.	Explosion
4.	Riot or civil commotion
5.	Aircraft, including self-propelled missiles and spacecraft
6.	Vehicles
7.	Smoke[b]
8.	Vandalism or malicious mischief
9.	Theft
10.	Falling objects[c]
11.	Weight of ice, snow, or sleet
12.	Accidental discharge or overflow of water or steam from within a plumbing, heating, air conditioning, or automatic fire-protective sprinkler system or from within a household appliance (with certain restrictions)
13.	Sudden and accidental tearing apart, cracking, burning, or bulging of a steam or hot water heating, air conditioning, or automatic fire protective sprinkler system, or an appliance for heating water[d]
14.	Freezing of a plumbing, heating, air conditioning, or automatic fire-protective sprinkler system or a household appliance if reasonable care has been used to maintain heat in the building or shut off the water supply and drain all systems and appliances of water[e]
15.	Sudden and accidental damage from artificially generated electrical current (with certain restrictions)
16.	Volcanic eruption, but not earthquake, land shock waves, or tremors

Source: ISO's HO-3 policy.

[a] Some states have established windstorm insurance pools as private insurers sometimes exclude coverage for wind-related damage. In addition, this specifically excludes from coverage damage caused by rain, snow, sleet, sand, and dust unless the wind or hail damage to the building permits those perils to enter.

[b] This only applies if it is sudden and accidental damage.

[c] This only covers property in a building if a building is also damaged by the falling object. However, damage to the fallen object itself is not covered.

[d] This does not include losses caused by or resulting from freezing.

[e] This does not include a sump, sump pump, roof drains, gutters, downspout, or other similar equipment.

When these criteria are generally satisfied, the insurer can add other expenses and profits to the expected losses and determine a price that is appropriate for the risk. Insurers may still decide to offer insurance for risks that deviate from these ideal characteristics. However, as one or more deviations occur, the ability of the insurer to estimate future losses decreases, the risk increases, and the insurer's capital is more exposed to inadequate prices for the coverage that the insurer offers.

Homeowners Policies Also Exclude Other Perils

Despite covering a range of perils, insurers also exclude a number of perils. Insurance companies may determine that a peril is uninsurable and exclude it from an insurance policy by inserting a provision that excludes coverage. These provisions can be located in different sections of a homeowners policy. For example, the HO-3 contains a section titled "Exclusions," but other policy provisions that exclude coverage are located elsewhere. Table 3 lists typical perils excluded under this section.

Other policy provisions that exclude coverage are located under "Perils Insured Against" in the HO-3 policy. Under this section, which applies to the dwelling and other structures, but not to personal property, damage caused by certain perils will not be covered (see table 4).

Insurers exclude these perils from homeowners policies for various reasons. According to some industry participants, some perils are excluded because they do not meet the criteria for insurable risks. For example, perils that result in catastrophic losses are generally infrequent, high-impact events that are difficult to predict and measure. The chances of these events occurring are difficult to calculate, and the losses can be so large and simultaneously impact so many homeowners that they could jeopardize a company's solvency because the insurer may not have sufficient capital to pay out the large number of claims. Examples of these types of risks include flood, earthquake, war, and nuclear hazard.

Table 3. Perils Listed in the Exclusions Section of the HO-3

1.	Ordinance or law (such as an ordinance or law requiring or regulating the construction, demolition, remodeling, renovation, or repair of property)
2.	Earth movement (such as earthquakes, landslides, mudslides, or sinkholes)[a]
3.	Water (including flood, waves, water which backs up through sewers or drains or overflows or is otherwise discharged from a sump, sump pump or related equipment, or water below the surface of the ground)[b]
4.	Power failure
5.	Neglect (failure to use reasonable means to save and preserve property at and after the time of loss)
6.	War
7.	Nuclear hazard
8.	Intentional loss (an action the insured commits or conspires to commit with intent to cause loss)
9.	Government action (such as the destruction, confiscation, or seizure of property by order of any governmental or public authority)[c]
10.	Weather conditions (only if the weather conditions contribute in any way with a cause or event excluded above to produce the loss)[d]
11.	Acts or decisions, including the failure to act or decide, of any person, group, organization, or governmental body[d]
12.	Faulty, inadequate or defective: planning, zoning, development, surveying, siting; design, specifications, workmanship, repair, construction, renovation, remodeling, grading, compaction; materials used in repair, construction, renovation, or remodeling; or maintenance[d]

Source: ISO's HO-3 policy.

[a] A direct loss by fire, explosion, or theft resulting from an earth movement is covered.

[b] A direct loss by fire, explosion, or theft resulting from water activity is covered.

[c] This excludes acts taken by the government at a time of a fire to prevent spread of the fire if the loss caused by the fire is covered under the policy.

[d] These three items are specific to dwellings and other structures.

Other risks are excluded because they could raise moral hazard issues if they were covered and because they are not accidental. Moral hazard is an increase in the probability of loss caused by the policyholder's behavior—for example, intentional loss, neglect, deterioration, and lack of maintenance. According to some industry participants, if these risks were covered, homeowners could, for example, neglect their roofs or not address mold problems and then file claims for replacement and remediation. Further they noted that these types of risks also fall outside the realm of insurance because they are not sudden or accidental and are generally unpredictable.

Some industry participants also said that homeowners policies list defective products as exclusions for a couple of reasons. First, they said that defective products are listed as exclusions because insurers would find it difficult and impractical to evaluate the wide range of manufactured products to determine the likelihood and extent of defects and price this risk for policies accordingly. Second, they suggested that manufacturers are responsible for defects in their products, and product warranties and commercial general liability insurance can help affected homeowners.[18] For example, some homeowners affected by defective drywall may receive compensation from settlements partly funded by commercial general liability insurance policies held by companies responsible for the distribution or installation of defective drywall.[19] Additionally, some homeowners impacted by defective drywall have filed insurance claims through their homeowners' insurance policies, and litigation in multiple states will determine the extent to which coverage for this drywall is covered by homeowners insurance.

Table 4. Other Excluded Perils for Dwellings and Other Structures Listed in the HO-3

1.	Collapse (including abrupt falling down or caving in; loss of structural integrity; or any cracking, bulging, sagging, bending, shrinking, leaning, settling, or expansions related to the falling or loss of structural integrity);
2.	Freezing of a plumbing, heating, air conditioning, or automatic fire-protective system or of a household appliance, or by discharge, leakage, or overflow from within the system or appliance caused by freezing, unless reasonable care has been used to maintain heat in the building or shut off the water supply and drain all systems and appliances of water;[a]
3.	Freezing, thawing, pressure, or weight of water or ice, whether driven by wind or not, to a fence, pavement, patio, swimming pool, and other listed structures;
4.	Theft in or to a dwelling under construction, or of materials and supplies for use in the construction until the dwelling is finished and occupied;
5.	Vandalism and malicious mischief and any ensuing loss caused by any intentional and wrongful act committed in the course of the vandalism or malicious mischief, if the dwelling has been vacant for more than 60 consecutive days immediately before the loss;
6.	Mold, fungus, or wet rot (except under certain circumstances); or
7.	Wear and tear, marring, deterioration; mechanical breakdown, latent defect, inherent vice, or any quality in property that causes it to damage or destroy itself; smog, rust, or other corrosion, or dry rot; smoke from agricultural smudging or industrial operations; discharge, dispersal, seepage, migration, release or escape of pollutants (except under certain circumstances); settling, shrinking, bulging or expansion, including resultant cracking, of bulkheads, pavements, patios, footings, foundations, walls, floors, roofs, or ceilings; birds, rodents, or insects; nesting or infestation, or discharge or release of waste products or secretions, by any animals; or animals owned or kept by an insured.

Source: ISO's HO-3 policy.

[a] The term plumbing does not include a sump, sump pump, roof drain, gutter, downspout, or similar equipment.

Coverage Depends on Several Factors, Including Policy Provisions and Location

Certain provisions found in homeowners policies can also affect coverage. Some industry participants cited as an example anticoncurrent causation clauses. For example, under these clauses, if damage is simultaneously caused by both an excluded peril (such as flood) and a covered peril (wind), coverage is excluded for that loss. They noted that these clauses presented a particular challenge for owners of coastal properties when hurricanes occurred. Cases challenging the enforceability of the anticoncurrent clause arose after the 2005 hurricane season because damage to properties may have resulted from a combination of high winds and flooding. According to reports, this clause may similarly become an issue for homeowners in the aftermath of Superstorm Sandy. In addition to the anticoncurrent causation clause, policies may also contain conditions that policyholders are required to comply with in order to maintain coverage. Under the HO-3 policy, for example, homeowners must provide prompt notice to their insurance company or agent following a loss and are also required to protect property from further damage once a loss has occurred. Failure to comply with these types of requirements may result in a loss of coverage.

In addition, the facts and conditions surrounding the loss event—including the cause of the damages and court decisions—may also impact coverage. For example, according to some industry participants, an HO-3 policy typically excludes mold damage. However, mold damage that is hidden within walls or ceilings, or beneath the floors of a structure, that results from the accidental discharge or overflow of water or steam from within a plumbing or heating system may be covered, among other things. Further, the HO-3 policy typically covers theft of personal property from a home. However, theft in a home that is under construction, for example, may not be covered. Court decisions may also impact coverage when disputes between policyholders and insurers end up in litigation, something that can take time to resolve. Ultimately, whether a loss is covered in these cases may depend on how the court interprets the policy. Following Hurricane Katrina, for example, some coverage disputes raised the question of whether a policy's flood exclusion language clearly excluded a water-related event, such as storm surge, that caused the damage at issue.[20]

Coverage may also depend on where homeowners live and whether they have purchased endorsements—optional coverage that alters a policy's terms and conditions that can be added at an additional cost—or have other insurance policies.[21] For example, homeowners policies typically do not cover flood damage, but flood insurance may be available through NFIP, depending on where a home is located.[22] Additionally, private insurers sometimes exclude coverage for wind-related damage to properties in coastal areas, requiring policyholders to either pay an additional premium for wind-related risks or purchase a supplemental policy for wind-related damages. In such cases, this supplemental coverage is typically provided by a state-sponsored wind insurance pool that has been created to address shortages in the availability of private insurance for wind-related risks. In Florida, for example, coverage is provided through its state insurance entity, the Citizens Property Insurance Corporation (Citizens).[23]

Earthquakes and sinkholes are two other perils that are also typically excluded from homeowners policies but that may be covered by a separate policy or an endorsement in some states. In California, for example, state law requires all residential property insurance companies to offer earthquake coverage to homeowners. In offering earthquake coverage, insurance companies can manage the risk themselves, contract with an affiliated or non-affiliated insurer, or become members of the California Earthquake Authority (CEA), a publicly-managed but privately funded entity that offers residential earthquake policies.[24] Similarly, sinkhole coverage is typically excluded under the earth movement exclusion found in standard homeowners policies, but in Florida, the state requires insurers to offer catastrophic ground cover collapse, which is a narrow form of coverage that protects against the total loss of a home due to sinkholes. Florida does not require any other sinkhole coverage to be included in homeowners policies, but insurers are required to offer additional sinkhole coverage. Homeowners in some states may also be able to purchase coverage through endorsements for other perils typically excluded from homeowners policies, including ordinance and law, sewer or drain backup, and mold.

Policy Exclusion Impacts Could Be Reduced by Expanding Homeowner Coverage, but Premiums Would Likely Increase

Losses due to policy exclusions can financially impact homeowners by causing significant out-of-pocket expenses. Communities can also be impacted by perils excluded from homeowners policies, particularly if unrepaired homes result in blight and affect whether others in a neighborhood rebuild. Expanded coverage could offer homeowners more protection, potentially reducing the cost of repairs that homeowners would have to cover with their own resources. However, policies that offered expanded coverage would likely be much more expensive than current policies.

Policy Exclusions Can Impact Homeowners and Communities

According to industry participants, the biggest and most significant impact on homeowners from policy exclusions is out-of-pocket costs to cover losses. If a loss occurs that is excluded by insurers, and coverage is not available through an endorsement or federal or state program, homeowners will have to use their own resources to rebuild and replace what they had. Some industry participants said that excluded losses can cause significant damage to homes and possessions. In some cases, homeowners may not have the means to rebuild after a disaster. Figures 1 and 2 illustrate the damage caused by two perils, floods and sinkholes, which are typically excluded from homeowners policies.

In addition to paying for excluded losses on their own, one industry organization said that homeowners may have to pay additional out-of- pocket expenses for temporary housing or a car rental that may not be covered by a homeowners policy.[25] When impacted by a disaster, homeowners may need these types of rentals for many months, and they can be costly.

Further, industry participants said that rebuilding after a disaster can present additional challenges for homeowners. One industry organization said that catastrophes can cause shortages of building contractors and building supplies that can delay reconstruction. This phenomenon is known as "demand surge." In these circumstances, the short-term costs of repairing and rebuilding homes can escalate substantially. Another industry participant noted that homeowners can also have their policies cancelled if home repairs are not adequate.

Disasters and excluded perils also sometimes highlight differences between consumers' expectations for insurance and actual policy coverage, resulting in added frustrations for homeowners. According to some industry participants with whom we spoke, some consumers may not learn what their policy actually covers until losses occur. For example, one industry association recalled that some consumers who had recent problems with drywall sourced from China filed insurance claims through their homeowners policies. As noted earlier, litigation in multiple states may determine the extent to which homeowners insurance applies to losses associated with this drywall.

Residential flooding examples. Above: Waynesville, MO. Right: Greenville, NC.

Source: FEMA.

Figure 1. Damage Due to Floods.

Sinkholes may range widely in terms of size and impact. The sinkhole in Winter Park, FL (above left) was eventually stabilized and turned into an urban lake by the city. In Bulan, KY (above right), a residential property is in danger of collapsing due to a sinkhole.

Source: National Oceanic and Atmospheric Administration (NOAA) National Geophysical Data Center (NGDC, A.S. Navory (left photo); FEMA (right photo).

Figure 2. Damage Due to Sinkholes.

Others may not understand their coverage well enough to know what is covered, what is excluded, and what loss events and circumstances might result in paid, partially paid, or denied claims. For example, according to a 2013 survey conducted by one industry organization, many homeowners mistakenly believe that their homeowners policies cover flooding from a hurricane.[26] According to some industry participants, homeowners policies can be difficult to understand because they often are long, technical, legal documents. One consumer advocate we spoke with suggested that few tools exist to help consumers understand their coverage, and noted that even though some states have policy readability requirements and disclosure rules about coverage and exclusions, these measures do not help consumers understand their policies. Other participants said that many homeowners do not read their policies or study them closely. Additional analysis would be needed to determine to what extent readability requirements, disclosure rules, or other factors impact homeowners' ability to understand their policies.

In addition to the devastation disasters may cause homeowners, neighborhoods and communities can also be impacted if some homeowners are unable to rebuild because they do not have coverage for a loss. Damaged homes that are not rebuilt can result in blight and affect the willingness of others to rebuild. A neighborhood where property is vacant or deteriorated will also likely impact the property value of surrounding homes. In addition, when some homeowners do not rebuild, communities may experience a diminution of the tax base. Collecting less in property taxes can impact the ability of communities to fund schools, libraries, parks, and roads, among other uses.

Government Coverage of Excluded Losses Can Involve Costs and Risks to Taxpayers

Both the federal and some state governments offer disaster assistance and other programs to help homeowners with some of the perils that private insurers do not cover, and this support can rely on taxpayer as well as policyholder resources. At the federal level, the government provides a range of assistance to individuals after major disasters. This assistance is generally made available after the President issues a disaster declaration under the authority of the Robert T. Stafford Disaster Relief and Emergency Assistance Act (the Stafford Act), and is administered by various federal agencies through various programs.[27] FEMA, for example, provides disaster relief and recovery assistance to individual citizens through its Individuals and Households Program (IHP), which is intended to provide money and services, including assistance in repairing and replacing damaged homes, to people in a disaster area when losses are not generally covered by insurance.[28] The growing number of major disaster declarations has contributed to an increase in federal expenditures for disaster assistance, however. For example, through January 31, 2012, FEMA obligated $80.3 billion in disaster relief, including $23.5 billion in individual assistance, for 539 disasters declared during fiscal years 2004 through 2011.[29] More recently, Superstorm Sandy has also involved significant federal disaster assistance. In January 2013, Congress passed and the President signed the Disaster Relief Appropriations Act of 2013 and the Sandy Recovery Improvement Act of 2013, which provided about $50 billion in federal assistance to support rebuilding efforts.[30]

In addition to providing disaster assistance, the federal government also offers flood insurance to homeowners through NFIP, a program that involves significant costs for the government and ultimately for taxpayers. According to FEMA information, as of September 2013, there were 5.6 million flood insurance policies in force in almost 22,000 communities across the United States. In years when losses were high, NFIP has used statutory authority to borrow funds from the Department of the Treasury (Treasury) to pay claims and keep the program solvent. For example, NFIP borrowed $16.8 billion from Treasury to cover claims for the 2005 hurricanes—primarily Hurricane Katrina—and received additional borrowing authority in the amount of $9.7 billion following Superstorm Sandy in 2012. As of October 2013, NFIP owed Treasury $24 billion. NFIP is generally expected to cover its claim payments and operating expenses with the premiums it collects. However, NFIP has sold some flood insurance policies at subsidized rates to help keep flood insurance affordable, and these subsidized policies have been a financial burden on the program because of their relatively high losses and premium rates that are not actuarially based. As a result, the annual amount that NFIP collects in both full-risk and subsidized premiums is generally not enough to cover its operating costs, claim payments, and principal and interest payments for the debt owed to Treasury, especially in years of catastrophic flooding, such as 2005.[31]

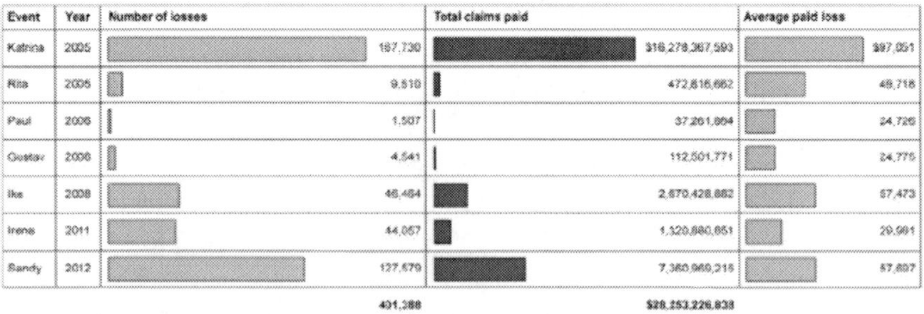

Source: FEMA.

Figure 3. Selected NFIP Flood Loss and Payment Information, 2005 to 2012.

This arrangement results in much of the financial risk of flooding being transferred to the federal government and ultimately the taxpayer. As shown in figure 3 below, NFIP has handled a significant number of claims and paid losses for flood events caused by hurricanes and a superstorm since 2005.[32]

Some states, such as Florida, have created residual insurance pools to cover what the private market will not, sometimes at a cost to policyholders and taxpayers across the state.[33] In Florida, Citizens provides homeowners coverage, including for wind damage, for those who cannot find coverage from private insurers. If Citizens' funds are depleted by paying claims after a catastrophic event, Florida law requires that Citizens charge assessments until any deficits are eliminated. Citizens' policyholders are the first to be assessed, and if necessary, additional assessments can be levied against certain private insurance companies, who can then pass the cost of these assessments on to their policyholders. [34] This ability to levy assessments provides Citizens with resources to pay claims to policyholders.

Storms in 2004 and 2005, for example, resulted in more than $30 billion in insured damage in Florida. Citizens sustained deficits of $515 million and $1.8 billion, respectively, in those years. To fund its 2004 deficit, Citizens assessed insurance companies and surplus lines policyholders over $515 million in regular assessments.[35] To fund the 2005 deficit, the Florida legislature appropriated $715 million from the Florida general revenue fund, reducing the size of the regular assessment from $878 million to $163 million. In 2005, the Florida legislature also directed Citizens to amortize the collection of the emergency assessment for the remaining $888 million deficit over a 10-year period, resulting in an emergency assessment levied beginning in June 2007. According to two industry organizations, Florida's property/casualty policyholders generally bear the cost of having Citizens provide coverage to participating Florida residents, regardless of whether they live inland or on the coast.

Expanding Private Coverage Could Offer Benefits, but Homeowner Premiums Would Likely Rise

If private insurers offered expanded homeowners coverage, homeowners could see a number of benefits. First, according to some industry participants homeowners would have more protection because more perils would be covered under their policy. Second, some industry participants noted that more comprehensive coverage could lead to less ambiguity for consumers seeking to understand their policies. Policies with fewer exclusions and conditions for coverage would be simpler and more efficient for insurers to write and consumers to understand than having separate policies for homeowners, flood, and in some states, wind coverage. Third, some industry participants said that enhanced coverage could reduce litigation and disputes between policyholders and insurers over coverage. For example, a policy that offered more comprehensive coverage could reduce disputes over the anticoncurrent causation clause, often over whether wind or water caused residential damage, something some industry participants noted is a particular challenge for homeowners when hurricanes occur.

Assuming homeowners purchased expanded private coverage without government subsidies, these policies could also reduce reliance on federal and state programs.[36] According to some industry participants, if homeowners policies covered flooding, for example, fewer taxpayer resources may be needed for paying NFIP's claims and subsidized premiums. In addition to having benefits at the federal level, greater private coverage could also reduce or eliminate the need for state-based insurance mechanisms, such as state wind pool coverage, and the insurer and policyholder assessments they can involve. Moreover, expanded coverage could encourage more informed decisions by homeowners. For instance, expanded coverage with more accurate pricing for risk could provide beneficial information to consumers on the risk associated with their housing location decisions and could encourage more consumers to mitigate risks to their property or to not locate to high- risk areas.

Notwithstanding these potential benefits, expanded coverage would likely increase insurance premiums for homeowners. According to some industry participants with whom we spoke, the increase could amount to several times what some homeowners currently pay. For example, one industry organization said that a policy that covered flood, earthquake, sinkholes, and some other perils could cost homeowners anywhere from three to five times what homeowners pay now, while another estimated that the cost of a policy that covered nearly all the currently excluded perils could exceed $15,000 annually. Other industry participants said the cost for this coverage would be so high that many homeowners would be unable to afford it. Additionally, FEMA information on the changes to the cost of flood insurance following the Biggert-Waters Act and the elimination of some subsidized rates may further illustrate how costly expanded coverage could potentially be for some homeowners. According to FEMA information, the cost of a NFIP policy for a home located in a very high-risk area without a subsidy could exceed $20,000 in annual premiums for certain policyholders.[37]

MULTIPLE CHALLENGES MAKE EXPANDING PRIVATE COVERAGE DIFFICULT

Several factors make it challenging for private insurers to offer all-perils homeowners insurance, or even more comprehensive policies. These include consumer demand for greater coverage and the higher premiums such coverage would involve, the ability of insurers to adequately price policies that covered more perils, and the regulatory challenges associated with getting approval for risk-based rates. A few industry participants with whom we spoke said that insurers and others are discussing possibilities for expanding private homeowners insurance, but cautioned that policy premium rate, affordability, and other conditions would need to be addressed.

Insurance Cost and Risk Pricing Are Issues for Consumers and Insurers

Consumer Demand and Incentives

Higher premiums for more comprehensive homeowners insurance are not only an affordability challenge for homeowners, they also represent a key challenge for insurers. Some industry participants said that the higher premiums required for more comprehensive coverage raises questions about whether sufficient demand would make expanded coverage impractical in the private market. Some said that many homeowners try to keep expenses for insurance as low as possible, citing as evidence low participation in NFIP, despite federal subsidies. They also questioned whether consumers would buy much more expensive expanded coverage even if it were offered by insurers.

Additionally, many industry participants with whom we spoke said that adverse selection—or the tendency for those who live in places most prone to risk to be most likely to purchase insurance—could challenge insurers' ability to expand policy coverage. Insurers manage risk by charging appropriate rates and diversifying their risk pool. Industry participants with whom we spoke said that if only riskier households—for example, those located near the coasts or rivers—were the primary purchasers of expanded coverage, insurers might end up with an insurance pool with concentrated risk and policies that could cause losses that may jeopardize insurers' profitability and solvency.

A requirement that insurers offer and homeowners purchase more comprehensive coverage may reduce this problem but raises questions about how such a requirement would be implemented.[38] Further, some questioned whether it would be fair to require those living in low-risk areas to purchase expanded coverage they may not need, in effect subsidizing those living in high-risk areas. One industry organization said that legislative or regulatory attempts to mandate all-perils coverage could destabilize the insurance marketplace in certain high-risk areas such as coastal regions and floodplains. It could also cause private insurers to further limit their exposures in disaster-prone areas, and some insurers may withdraw from the market altogether. Industry participants suggested that offering policies that covered all losses could also raise issues of moral hazard, or incentivize risky behavior by homeowners. For example, comprehensive policies may encourage people to locate their homes in high-risk areas. Others said that higher premiums associated with more comprehensive policies would send a better signal to homeowners about the risk associated with their housing location, something that could prompt homeowners to properly insure their homes or take steps to mitigate their risk.

Risk Pricing and Claims Processing

Industry participants said that another important challenge is the difficulty of pricing catastrophic risks and handling the claims that they cause. Some industry participants said that accurately modeling the broader range of risks that more comprehensive policies would cover was critically important. Having loss data and accurately modeling risk is necessary for appropriately pricing insurance policies and for ensuring insurer solvency. Some industry participants said that because expanded coverage would be new to the private domestic market, modeling experience would need to be developed over time and could be challenging, particularly for multiple catastrophic losses. Others said that insurers might also lack the expertise to handle claims for perils that were typically excluded, and that it could take time for insurers and adjusters to develop the expertise to handle some disaster situations and subsequent claims.

Approval for Risk-based Rates and Insurer Capital Pose Additional Concerns

Regulatory Rate Approval

Industry participants said that insurers could also face critical regulatory challenges in offering more comprehensive coverage. One important challenge is that state regulatory approval for the higher premiums more comprehensive coverage would likely demand is uncertain. Insurers need to charge risk-based rates that are determined on an actuarial basis in order to stay solvent and meet their policy obligations to homeowners. However, some industry participants with whom we spoke said that getting regulators to approve rates that insurers determined would be appropriate for certain risks has been difficult and that getting approval for rates that could be several times more expensive than those currently in force would be an important challenge. One regulator, however, said that inability to charge higher risk-based rates might not be an issue because loss experience is a critical factor that drives rates. If insurers faced greater losses by covering more perils, they would likely be able to justify and gain approval for higher premiums. Industry participants also said that different state insurance laws and regulations and different rate- setting and approval processes could make it difficult for insurers to sell more comprehensive policies with risk-based rates across states.

Insurer Capital

Offering coverage for a broader set of perils would also require insurers to have the capital necessary to pay claims without risking insolvency. The greater the risk, the more capital insurers need to hold. Insurers may not be willing to maintain the higher capital levels needed for insuring against higher risk events if that capital could be used for other insurance or investment purposes. In addition, disasters such as floods and earthquakes are relatively infrequent but often severe events, so that insurers cannot always know how much they will need in reserves. Industry participants said that the unpredictability of catastrophes could prevent insurers from accurately calculating and setting aside the sums necessary to cover losses. One insurance regulator suggested that even if insurers could charge rates that reflected the full risk of disasters, they still may not be able to offer coverage for additional perils.

Several Conditions Would Be Needed for Insurers to Expand Private Coverage

For additional coverage to be possible, insurers would need the ability to conduct actuarial analyses and accurately model risks involved with greater homeowners coverage. Some industry participants thought this capability may already exist or could be developed for floods and earthquakes, the two perils they said hold some promise for greater private insurer involvement. In order to offer coverage for flood or other perils, insurers would have to be able to charge risk-based rates, a critical part of meeting their policy obligations to consumers and staying solvent, but something that would also raise concerns about higher premium costs, policy affordability, and consumer demand.

Two industry organizations said that mitigation efforts, effective building codes, and sound land-use policies could also help reduce risks from natural catastrophes. Another highlighted how building codes set by states can differ, which can lead to inconsistencies that make it difficult to ensure properties can withstand loss events. Others said that it is important for the insurance industry to encourage consumers to become better informed about their risks and insurance so that they could take available steps depending on where they live to mitigate losses.

The catastrophic nature of flood and other natural catastrophe losses, according to industry participants, may require a continuing role for federal and state government in financing coverage. We recently reported on strategies to encourage greater private-sector involvement in flood insurance that included the possibility of insurers charging homeowners full risk rates with the government providing targeted subsidies to help with affordability. Private insurers could play a greater role in coverage with the federal government possibly serving as an insurer for only the highest risk properties. Yet another option is the combination of greater private-sector involvement and the government acting as a reinsurer by providing a backstop to private insurers for losses over a certain amount.[39]

The size of the losses and the magnitude of the risk associated with more comprehensive policies underscore the complex challenges of addressing the costs of catastrophes and other perils that place homeowners' properties at risk. A mix of factors—financial risk, large potential losses, political and regulatory issues, policy affordability, and consumer demand—has thus far made it challenging for private-sector insurers in the U.S. to offer flood insurance to homeowners, let alone more comprehensive or all-perils policies. The possibility of improved data, better risk modeling, and emerging private-sector interest, however, suggest that some additional coverage may be possible. For this to happen, private insurers must be able to assess and diversify risk and charge rates adequate for the risk they are assuming. At the same time, consumers will need to better recognize the risk and cost of their housing decisions and the likely higher rates that come with protecting homes and possessions in certain locations. One of the most fundamental challenges is achieving a policy premium rate that allows insurers to stay solvent and meet their obligations to consumers, yet is affordable enough so that consumers are willing and able to buy insurance. Addressing this important challenge and ensuring a collective response to losses caused by disasters and other perils will require the cooperation and resources of government, homeowners, and insurers, as well as balance in the assumption of risk and cost by each of these parties.

AGENCY COMMENTS

We provided a draft of this report for review and comment to the National Association of Insurance Commissioners (NAIC) and the Federal Insurance Office (FIO) at the Department of the Treasury. Both provided technical comments which we incorporated into the report as appropriate.

Alicia Puente Cackley
Director, Financial Markets and Community Investment

APPENDIX I: OBJECTIVES, SCOPE, AND METHODOLOGY

In this report we examined (1) the perils homeowners policies typically cover and exclude; (2) the impacts of exclusions on homeowners and taxpayers and the potential benefits of more comprehensive coverage for homeowners; and (3) the additional perils insurers might be willing to cover and the challenges associated with such coverage.

To determine what perils homeowners policies typically cover and exclude, we analyzed the Insurance Services Office's (ISO) standard homeowners insurance policy (HO-3) and examples of private insurers' homeowners policies. We reviewed documents by insurance industry organizations and professional associations, including the National Association of Insurance Commissioners (NAIC) and the Insurance Information Institute (III). We also interviewed a nongeneralizable, judgmental sample of property/casualty insurance companies and state insurance regulators, insurance and reinsurance associations, an insurance agent and broker association, consumer groups, academic insurance and risk experts, and the Federal Insurance Office (FIO) at the Department of the Treasury. We selected our sample of insurers based on market share by direct premiums underwritten and participation in different geographic markets. We selected our sample of state regulators based on geographic diversity and experience overseeing insurers with portfolios of different perils, including floods, hurricanes, and earthquakes.

To determine the impacts of exclusions on homeowners and taxpayers and the benefits of more comprehensive coverage, we spoke with consumer groups, including the Center for Economic Justice, academic experts, selected state insurance regulators, NAIC and FIO officials, and other insurance association officials. To illustrate some of the financial impacts of policy exclusions on taxpayers, we obtained publicly available data from the Federal Emergency Management Agency (FEMA) on the National Flood Insurance Program's (NFIP) claims costs. For the NFIP data we used, we interviewed officials on usability and reliability. We determined that these data were sufficiently reliable for our intended purposes. In addition, we reviewed our previous work on natural catastrophe insurance, academic and other studies, and results from an annual survey conducted by Insurance Information Institute (III) on homeowners insurance, flood insurance, and disaster preparedness.

To identify the additional perils that insurers might be willing to insure and the challenges associated with such coverage, we spoke with a sample of insurance companies and state insurance regulators, insurance and reinsurance associations, an insurance agent and broker association, NAIC and FIO officials, consumer groups, academia, and others. We also reviewed our previous work on natural catastrophe insurance, Congressional Research Service (CRS) reviews, and academic and other studies on these issues. We gathered additional perspectives on all perils policies from a round table discussion on privatizing flood insurance that we organized and conducted at GAO headquarters in Washington, D.C. Participants in the round table included insurance industry association representatives, select state regulators, and NAIC and FEMA officials.

We conducted this performance audit from December 2012 to January 2014 in accordance with generally accepted government auditing standards. Those standards require that we plan and perform the audit to obtain sufficient, appropriate evidence to provide a reasonable basis for our findings and conclusions based on our audit objectives. We believe that the evidence obtained provides a reasonable basis for our findings and conclusions based on our audit objectives.

APPENDIX II: INFORMATION ON THE NATIONAL FLOOD INSURANCE PROGRAM

Established in 1968, the National Flood Insurance Program (NFIP) makes federally backed flood insurance available to residential property owners and to owners of nonresidential property such as businesses, churches, governments and nonprofits. Under NFIP, the federal government generally assumes the liability for the insurance coverage and sets rates and coverage limitations, among other responsibilities, while the private insurance industry sells the policies and administers the claims[40] The Federal Emergency Management Agency (FEMA) is responsible for administering NFIP.

Community participation in NFIP is voluntary. However, communities must join NFIP and adopt FEMA-approved building standards and floodplain management strategies in order for their residents to purchase flood insurance through the program. Additionally, communities with Special Flood Hazard Areas (SFHA)—areas at high risk for flooding— must participate in NFIP to be eligible for any form of assistance for acquisition or construction purposes in connection with a flood.[41] Participating communities can receive credits on premium rates on flood insurance if they establish floodplain management programs that go beyond the minimum requirements of NFIP. FEMA can suspend communities that do not comply with the program, and communities can withdraw from the program. As of September 2013, almost 22,000 communities voluntarily participated in NFIP.

Consumers can purchase flood insurance to cover both buildings and contents for residential and commercial properties. NFIP's maximum coverage for residential policyholders is $250,000 for building property and $100,000 for contents. This coverage includes replacement value of the building and its foundation, electrical and plumbing systems, central air and heating, furnaces and water heater, and equipment considered part of the overall structure of the building. Personal property coverage includes clothing, furniture, and portable electronic equipment. For commercial policyholders, the maximum coverage is $500,000 per unit for buildings and $500,000 for contents (for items similar to those covered under residential policies).[42] Coverage for personal property and coverage for nonresidential buildings is written on an actual cash value basis.

NFIP offers two types of flood insurance premiums to property owners who live in participating communities: subsidized and full-risk. The National Flood Insurance Act of 1968 authorized NFIP to offer subsidized premiums to owners of certain properties. Congress originally mandated the use of subsidized premiums to encourage communities to join the program and mitigate concerns that charging rates that fully and accurately reflected flood risk would be a burden to some property owners. According to FEMA, Congress made changes to the program over the years to encourage further participation in NFIP through low premiums. FEMA estimated that in 2012 more than 1 million of its residential flood insurance policies—about 20 percent—were sold at subsidized rates; nearly all were located in high-risk flood areas.[43]

Since 2000, NFIP has experienced several years with catastrophic losses—losses exceeding $1 billion—and has needed to borrow money from the Treasury to cover claims in some years. The losses resulting from Superstorm Sandy, which caused extensive damage in several states on the eastern coast of the United States in October 2012, also are catastrophic, reaching over $7 billion. As of October 2013, FEMA owed Treasury $24 billion. As a result of the program's importance, level of indebtedness to Treasury, substantial financial exposure for the federal government and taxpayers, and FEMA's management challenges, NFIP has been on our high-risk list since 2006.[44]

APPENDIX III: INFORMATION ON THE CITIZENS PROPERTY INSURANCE CORPORATION

Established in 2002, Florida Citizens Property Insurance Corporation (Citizens) is a not-for-profit and tax-exempt government entity that provides property insurance to homes and businesses that cannot get coverage in the private sector.[45] It consolidated two residual market mechanisms: the Florida Windstorm Underwriting Association (FWUA), created in 1970 to provide high-risk, windstorm, and hail residual market coverage in select areas of Florida, and the Florida Residential Property and Casualty Joint Underwriting Association (JUA), created in December 1992 following Hurricane Andrew to provide residual market residential-property multiperil insurance coverage, excluding wind if the property was within FWUA-eligible areas. A primary driver for the merger was that the combined entity obtained federally tax-exempt status, allowing it to save federal income taxes that otherwise would have been paid by FWUA and JUA.[46] As an integral part of the state rather than a private insurance company, Citizens is also able to issue tax-exempt post-event bonds and taxable pre-event bonds, which can help finance loss payments in the event of a major disaster.

Florida law determines the standards Citizens uses to establish its premium rates. Citizens' rates are required to be actuarially sound, but at the beginning of 2007, an approved rate increase was rescinded and rate levels were frozen by the Florida legislature at the 2006 rate levels. The rate freeze remained in effect through December 31, 2009. On January 1, 2010, Citizens began implementation of a statutorily required path to achieve actuarially sound rates over time. Except for sinkhole coverage, the path limits annual rate increases to 10 percent for any single policy issued by the corporation, excluding coverage changes and surcharges. According to Citizens officials, Citizens' rates are moving towards actuarial soundness, but are not yet there.

Citizens allocates approximately 18 percent of every premium dollar it collects to pay hurricane and catastrophe claims, but in the event that losses exceed its surplus, it is required by statute to levy assessments to recover the deficit. Assessments can be charged in up to three tiers, policyholder surcharge, regular, and emergency. Each additional tier is charged only if the level before is insufficient to eliminate Citizens' deficit. Citizens' policyholder surcharge is the first tier of assessments and can be levied one time for up to 45 percent of the policyholder's premium in a single year. If a deficit remains in one of Citizens' three types of accounts, Citizens can levy regular assessments of up to two percent against certain private insurance companies, who can then pass the cost of these assessments on to their policyholders.[47] Finally, if a deficit persists, Citizens can impose an emergency assessment on both Citizens and non-Citizens policyholders.[48] This ability to levy assessments provides Citizens with resources to pay claims to policyholders. For example, following the 2004 storms, Citizens had to levy over $515 million in regular assessments to fund its deficit.

Citizens' resources also come from its reinsurance arrangement with the Florida Hurricane Catastrophe Fund (FHCF). Established in 1993 by the Florida legislature, FHCF is a state-run reinsurer created to provide additional insurance capacity and help stabilize the property insurance market by reimbursing insurers for a portion of their catastrophic hurricane losses. As a tax-exempt entity, FHCF can accumulate premium payments on a tax-free basis. If the revenue generated from premiums is insufficient following a loss event, FHCF, like Citizens, is required by state law to levy assessments on a broad base of property/casualty insurance lines to fund revenue bonds to pay the losses. For example, FHCF issued bonds in the amount of $1.35 billion in

2006 and $625 million in 2008, which are being financed by a 1 percent assessment levied on property/casualty insurers in the state.

As of October 2013, Citizens had more than 1.2 million policies in force, most of which were homeowners policies. According to a Citizens official, Citizens has recently engaged in depopulation efforts by seeking ways to return policies to the private market, but these efforts have been met with challenges. For example, Citizens has faced challenges with establishing rates higher than those available in the private market. The insurance distribution process is also a challenge. For example, according to a Citizens official, private insurers that decline to sell a homeowner a policy may refer that homeowner to Citizens instead of recommending they shop the market for coverage, which has impeded a freely competitive insurance market.

APPENDIX IV: INFORMATION ON THE CALIFORNIA EARTHQUAKE AUTHORITY

Established in 1996, the California Earthquake Authority (CEA) is an instrumentality of the state that sells earthquake insurance policies for residential property throughout California. CEA is a publicly managed, privately funded entity. After the Northridge Earthquake that struck the San Fernando Valley in January 1994, insurers in California began to limit their exposure to earthquakes by writing fewer or no new homeowners insurance policies.[49] In 1995, California lawmakers passed a bill that allowed insurers to offer a reduced-coverage earthquake insurance policy. In offering earthquake coverage, insurance companies can manage the risk themselves, contract with an affiliated or non-affiliated insurer, or become a CEA-participating insurance company and offer CEA's residential earthquake policies. CEA is the largest earthquake insurer in California, with approximately 840,000 policies in force as of 2011, which represent approximately 70 percent of the residential earthquake insurance policies in the state.

CEA offers a basic residential earthquake policy to homeowners, which includes coverage for the insured dwelling and limited coverage for contents and loss-of-use if the residence is uninhabitable due to an earthquake. For an additional premium, CEA policyholders can significantly increase insured limits on contents and for loss-of-use, and homeowners can lower their CEA policy deductible from 15 percent to 10 percent.[50] CEA coverage is available to homeowners only from the insurance company that provides their residential property insurance and only if that company is a CEA-participating insurance company. Participating insurance companies process all CEA policy applications, policy renewals, invoices, and payments and handle all CEA claims.

In determining premium rates, CEA is required by law to use the best science available and is permitted by law to use earthquake computer modeling, to establish actuarially sound rates. CEA will examine rating factors, such as the rating territory (determined by ZIP code), age, and type of construction of a home, in determining the premium rate.[51] The CEA governing board establishes premium rates, subject to the prior approval of the Insurance Commissioner. In 2011, for example, a request for a 12.5 percent average statewide rate decrease was approved beginning with new and renewal policies that became effective on and after January 1, 2012. The change was a result of a reduction in the estimated average annual loss, as derived from new scientific information, according to CEA information. Given that the rate decrease is expressed as an average statewide rate impact, individual policyholders may have seen their rates increase or decrease, depending on CEA product, location of the risk, and other rating factors.

CEA is funded principally from policyholder premiums, contributions from and assessments on participating insurers, returns on invested funds, borrowed funds, and reinsurance. Assessments on participating insurers may not be directly passed through to policyholders. CEA is authorized to issue bonds, and may not cease to exist so long as its bonds are outstanding. As of 2012, CEA had approximately $10.2 billion in claims- paying capacity, but if an earthquake causes insured damage greater than CEA's claims-paying capacity, then policyholders affected will be paid a prorated portion of their covered losses or may be paid in installments.

End Notes

[1] A peril is a specific risk or event that may cause a loss.

[2] National Oceanic and Atmospheric Administration, *National Coastal Population Report: Population Trends from 1970 to 2020* (Washington, D.C.: Mar. 2013).

[3] For the purposes of this report, "industry participants" refers to those entities with a role in the insurance industry, including regulators, consumer advocates, industry associations, insurance company officials, and academic experts.

[4] Additional living expenses are extra charges covered by homeowners policies over and above the policyholder's customary living expenses. They kick in when the policyholder requires temporary shelter due to damage by a covered peril that makes the home temporarily uninhabitable.

[5] See National Association of Insurance Commissioners (NAIC), *A Consumer's Guide to Home Insurance* (Kansas City, MO: 2010) and Insurance Information Institute (III), *Insurance Handbook: A Guide to Insurance: What it Does and How it Works* (New York, N.Y.: 2010).

[6] The amount of coverage available under a homeowners policy is subject to limits, which are the maximum amounts the insurance policy will pay in the event of a loss. The limit for the dwelling is typically selected by the policyholder. The limits for other structures, personal property, and loss of use are expressed as percentages of the dwelling limit.

[7] According to industry participants, the valuation method used to determine the value of a home depends on the language in the insurance policy. For example, the home's value may be determined by the insurer or may be based on an appraisal. Each structure may also require a different valuation method.

[8] See NAIC, *A Consumer's Guide to Home Insurance* and III, *Insurance Handbook: A Guide to Insurance: What it Does and How it Works.*

[9] According to information from a state insurance department, many insurance companies require policyholders to purchase coverage for at least 80 percent of the home's replacement cost, and some require 100 percent. If a homeowner is underinsured and suffers a total loss, the homeowner may be reimbursed up to the coverage limit the homeowner purchased.

[10] The federal government retains the authority to regulate insurance, but has given primary responsibility for insurance regulation to the states in accordance with the McCarran-Ferguson Act of 1945. See Pub. L. No. 79-5, ch. 20, 59 Stat. 33 (1945) codified as amended at 15 U.S.C. §§ 1011-1015. See also GAO, *Ultimate Effects of McCarran- Ferguson Federal Antitrust Exemption on Insurer Activity Are Unclear*, GAO-05-816R (Washington, D.C.: July 28, 2005). Nevertheless, the federal government is involved in a wide range of areas with respect to the insurance sector, including operation of the National Flood Insurance Program, and crop and terrorism insurance programs. In addition, the Federal Reserve Board supervises insurers designated by the Financial Stability Oversight Council.

[11] Examples of wind risks include hurricanes and tornadoes.

[12] Pub. L. No. 90-448, Title XIII, § 1302, 82 Stat. 476, 572 (1968).

[13] FEMA is part of the Department of Homeland Security.

[14] For more information on NFIP, see Appendix II and recent GAO work, including GAO, *Flood Insurance: Implications of Changing Coverage Limits and Expanding Coverage,* GAO-13-568 *(Washington, D.C.: July 3, 2013); Flood Insurance: More Information Needed on Subsidized Properties,* GAO-13-607 *(Washington, D.C.: July 3, 2013) and Flood Insurance: Strategies for Increasing Private Sector Involvement*, GAO-14-127 (Washington, D.C.: Jan. 22, 2014).

[15] In addition to providing data and analytics services, ISO develops standard insurance policy language for use in the insurance industry. According to some industry participants, insurers may develop their own proprietary policies that deviate from the HO-3, but the covered perils and exclusions in those policies typically remain the same.

[16] For more information on insurable risk criteria, see GAO, *Terrorism Insurance: Measuring and Predicting Losses from Unconventional Weapons Is Difficult, but Some Industry Exposure Exists*, GAO-06-1081 (Washington, D.C.: Sept. 25, 2006) and George E. Rejda, *Principles of Risk Management and Insurance,* 8th ed. (Boston, Mass.: Pearson Education, Inc., 2003).

[17] Alternatively, a catastrophic loss is one that is extraordinarily large relative to the number of properties at risk in a given insurance pool.

[18] Commercial general liability insurance is a standard insurance policy issued to business organizations to protect them against liability claims for bodily injury and property damage arising out of premises, operations, products, and completed operations, as well as advertising and personal injury liability.

[19] For more information on defective drywall and alternative methods of providing relief from damage associated with it, see GAO, *Information on Defective Drywall,* GAO-13-735R (Washington, D.C.: July 31, 2013).

[20] For more information on wind and flood damage determinations following Hurricane Katrina, see GAO, *National Flood Insurance Program: Greater Transparency and Oversight of Wind and Flood Damage Determinations Are Needed*, GAO-08-28 (Washington, D.C.: Dec. 28, 2007).

[21] An endorsement is sometimes called a rider. In addition to buying back coverage for certain risks, endorsements can also be used by insurers to limit coverage in a policy.

[22] Some property owners may also purchase excess flood insurance from private insurers if the value of their home exceeds the coverage limits offered by NFIP.

[23] Citizens is a not-for-profit, tax-exempt government corporation that provides insurance protection to Florida property owners throughout the state. The corporation insures hundreds of thousands of homes, businesses, and condominiums whose owners otherwise might not be able to find coverage. For more information on Citizens, see appendix III.

[24] The base CEA policy, known as a "mini-policy," is a reduced-coverage, catastrophic earthquake insurance policy intended to protect a dwelling, while excluding coverage for costly nonessential items, such as swimming pools, patios, and detached structures. For more information about CEA and other state insurance entities, see appendix IV and GAO, *Natural Disasters: Public Policy Options for Changing the Federal Role in Natural Catastrophe Insurance,* GAO-08-7 (Washington, D.C.: Nov. 26, 2007).

[25] Some industry participants have emphasized that data to quantify out-of-pocket losses due to excluded perils are currently unavailable because insurers generally track the amounts they pay out in claims but not uninsured loss amounts.

[26] According to the Insurance Information Institute's 2013 Annual Pulse Survey, about 21 percent of the public believes flooding from a hurricane is covered. This proportion rises by 8 percentage points in the south, an area of the United States typically impacted by hurricanes.

[27] The Stafford Act is codified as amended at 42 U.S.C. § 5121 et seq. Federal disaster assistance is also provided to state, territorial, and local governments as well as nongovernmental entities.

[28] For more information on federal disaster assistance for individuals and households, see GAO-08-7. The Stafford Act specifies that federal agencies providing financial assistance after a major disaster cannot provide assistance to an individual for the same loss for which another federal program or private insurance company has provided compensation.

[29] GAO, *Federal Disaster Assistance: Improved Criteria Needed to Assess a Jurisdiction's Capability to Respond and Recover on Its Own,* GAO-12-838 (Washington, D.C.: Sept. 12, 2012).

[30] For more information on these rebuilding efforts, see Hurricane Sandy Rebuilding Task Force, *Hurricane Sandy Rebuilding Strategy: Stronger Communities, A Resilient Region* (Washington, D.C.: Aug. 2013).

[31] The Biggert-Waters Flood Insurance Reform Act of 2012 (Biggert-Waters Act) reauthorized NFIP through 2017 and made some significant changes to the program, such as eliminating premium subsidies for certain properties, creating a reserve fund, and eliminating the grandfathering of properties to old rates after remapping. However, implementation of certain changes was delayed by provisions in the Consolidated Appropriations Act, 2014. While these Biggert-Waters Act changes may help increase NFIP's long-term financial stability when they are implemented, the program still faces challenges in implementing the changes and their ultimate effect is not yet known. Biggert- Waters Flood Insurance Reform Act of 2012, Pub. L. No. 112-141, 126 Stat. 405, 916 (2012). See also GAO-13-568 and GAO, *National Flood Insurance Program: Continued Attention Needed to Address Challenges,* GAO-13-858T (Washington, D.C.: Sept. 18, 2013).

[32] Data are current as of September 30, 2013.

[33] Residual insurance pools serve as a coverage source of last resort for firms and individuals unable to find insurance offered by private market insurers. Residual markets require insurers writing specific coverage lines in a given state to assume the profits or losses

accruing from insuring that state's residual risks in proportion to their share of the total voluntary market premiums written in that state.

[34] Citizens has three types of internal accounts: Personal lines account (for personal residential policies); Commercial lines account (for commercial residential and nonresidential policies); and Coastal account (for personal residential policies and commercial residential and commercial nonresidential policies issued by Citizens, which provide coverage for the peril of wind in certain designated areas. Citizens can levy three types of assessments: policyholder surcharge, regular, and emergency. Citizens' policyholders are the first to be assessed if a deficit occurs. It is a one-time surcharge of up to 45 percent of the policyholder's premium depending on the deficit size. For the Coastal account, if a deficit remains after the policyholder assessment, Citizens can levy regular assessments that include a broad base of licensed Florida property/casualty insurance companies. The insurers may recoup this assessment amount by passing it on to policyholders. Finally if deficits still remain for the coastal account or if any deficit remains after the policyholder assessment for the personal and commercial lines accounts, a broad range of property/casualty policyholders, including Citizens policyholders, are assessed directly by their insurance companies. For each account, this assessment can be up to 10 percent of the amount needed to cover the deficit or 10 percent of the aggregate statewide direct written premium for the subject lines of business and all accounts of the corporation for the prior year–plus for both interest, fees, commissions, required reserves, and other costs.

[35] The term "surplus lines" refers to any type of insurance for which there is no available market within a state and which the state allows nonadmitted insurers to offer. A nonadmitted insurer is not licensed to do standard business in the state.

[36] Although one industry participant we spoke with suggested that expanding private coverage for perils such as mold and nuclear hazard may be possible, most participants discussed the possibility of expanding private coverage for natural catastrophes, such as flood and earthquakes. According to one participant, industry discussions about expanding homeowners coverage tend to center on natural catastrophes because these are the perils that most affect homeowners.

[37] Information is as of October 2013.

[38] As we previously reported, requiring insurers to offer an all-perils policy could be challenging. It is unclear how private insurers would be encouraged to underwrite all risks and it might not be cost effective for the federal government if low-income residents require government subsidies to address affordability issues. If expanded coverage did not sufficiently reduce post event disaster relief, these subsidies could cause significant costs for taxpayers. Furthermore, such a requirement could be challenging for the federal government to enforce, as has been seen with mandatory flood insurance in communities in designated floodplains. See GAO-08-7.

[39] See GAO-14-127.

[40] Some of these same insurers also provide coverage for flood insurance above the limit of NFIP coverage. A number of private insurers that do not sell and administer NFIP policies also offer flood insurance. Flood insurance purchased above current NFIP coverage limits generally is referred to as excess flood insurance.

[41] The National Flood Insurance Reform Act of 1994 requires individuals, including in SFHAs, who receive disaster assistance for flood disaster losses to real or personal property to purchase and maintain flood insurance coverage for as long as they live in the dwelling.

[42] For information on the implications of changing coverage limits and expanding coverage, see GAO, *Flood Insurance: Implications of Changing Coverage Limits and Expanding Coverage*, GAO-13-568 (Washington, D.C.: July 3, 2013).

[43] The Biggert-Waters Flood Insurance Reform Act of 2012 (Biggert-Waters Act) introduced many changes intended to strengthen the future solvency of NFIP. In particular, the act eliminated subsidized premium rates for several types of properties. However, certain changes were delayed by provisions in the Consolidated Appropriations Act, 2014. For

more information on subsidized properties, see GAO, *Flood Insurance: More Information Needed on Subsidized Properties*, GAO-13-607 (Washington, D.C.: July 3, 2013).

[44] GAO regularly reports on government operations that it identifies as high risk. For the most recent high risk report, see GAO, *High-Risk Series: An Update*, GAO-13-283 (Washington, D.C.: Feb. 2013).

[45] State government insurance programs, like Citizens, have typically been created after disasters because homeowners insurance coverage for catastrophic events is often not available from private insurers at prices deemed affordable by state legislators and insurance regulators.

[46] The merger also resulted in some overhead cost savings by having a single organization.

[47] Citizens has three types of internal accounts: Personal lines account (for personal residential policies); Commercial lines account (for commercial residential and nonresidential policies); and Coastal account (for personal residential policies and commercial residential and commercial nonresidential policies issued by Citizens which provides coverage for the peril of wind on risk that is located in areas eligible for coverage by the Florida Windstorm Association). The regular assessment is only applicable to the coastal account, and can be levied on private-market policyholders, including but not limited to homeowners, auto, and specialty and surplus lines policies.

[48] This assessment can be charged at a rate of up to 30 percent of premium (up to 10 percent per account with a deficit) per year until any remaining deficit is eliminated.

[49] California insurers had collected $3.4 billion in earthquake premiums in the 25-year period prior to the Northridge Earthquake and paid out more than $15 billion on Northridge claims alone.

[50] In July 2011, the "Homeowners Choice" product was approved and became available to consumers beginning July 1, 2012. According to CEA information, this product enhances availability and affordability as it offers more choice in coverage options and allows consumers to manage their residential earthquake insurance premium.

[51] CEA applies a 5 percent premium discount to dwellings that meet the following requirements: the dwelling was built before 1979, the frame is tied to the foundation, it has cripple walls braced with plywood or its equivalent, and the water heater is secured to the building frame.

INDEX

D

E

F

S

T

U

V

W

Y